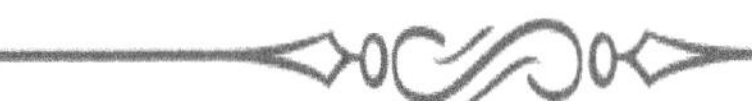

This, That, and Other Miracles

Inspirational Short Stories of Answered Prayers

Shirley Alberta Roberts Combs

To order additional copies of this book, contact:

Shirley Combs
733 N.E. 18th Street
Moore, Oklahoma 73160

Published by Shirley A. Combs

Editor, Layout and Cover Design:
FWB Publications, Columbus, Ohio

ISBN: 9798615670107 Soft Cover | Prayer | Missions

TABLE OF CONTENTS

DEDICATION

To my missionary co-laborers who served with us in Brazil, South America, and to their children who made an impact as they worked alongside their parents.

At this writing, about sixteen have already passed on to glory and have met face-to-face the Lord of the Harvest that commissioned them to go into all the world.

<u>Families</u>
Dave and Pat Franks – *Ken and *Marvis Eagleton
Bobby and *Geneva Poole –*Sam and June Wilkinson
Bobby and Sue Aycock – Earnie and *Willie Jean Deeds
*Jim and Shirley Combs – Don and *Carol Robirds
Walter and Marcia Ellison – *Louis and Florine Coscia
Tom and Nancy Hughes -*John and Connie Craft
Jim and Vickie Sturgill – Jim and Susan Moser
Norman and Laura McFall - Curt and Mary Holland
David and Annette Aycock - Andrew and Andrea Moore
*Terry and Jaime Eagleton - Kenneth and Rejane Eagleton

<u>Lady Warriors</u>
*Eula Mae Martin (Fornel), Nurse – *Esther Ruehle, Nurse
*Mary Ellen Rice, Child Evangelism
Kimberly Johnson ((Almeira), Social Worker

<u>Second Generation Missionaries (M.K.)</u>
David Aycock – *Terry Eagleton – Kenneth Eagleton
John Poole - Daniel Deeds
<u>Appointed-Never arrived</u>
*John and *Kay Metcalf
Kristen Wilson

* Deceased, in Glory!

Brazil Annual Field Council

ACKNOWLEDGEMENTS

Once again I thank my readers and participants in my seminars and classes for encouraging me to continue to record inspirational, and true stories that I have been blessed to experience.

And I give thanks to the Holy Spirit for nudging me to compile them into book form. (I was reluctant, claiming that it was a lot of hard work and expensive.) He seemed to impress upon me that the wonders and miracles that thrilled me and built my faith were not for me alone, but that I must continue to share them with others through the written word for His
Glory.

My friend and publisher, Alton Loveless, has been a help with his years of professional experiences, with his sharing my FWB roots, with his vision to get inspirational stories and information out in written form, with his kind words as we both travel our new-normal journeys through recent widowhood, and with his first-hand knowledge visit to my beloved Brazil.

A special thanks to my sister-in-law, Judith A. Combs Puckett, and to my son, Kemper, for helping to edit page after page to put these stories into a more meaningful way. My granddaughter, Julia, patiently walked me through the wonders of computers and photos.

I acknowledge that it is my Lord who uses the ordinary to do the extraordinary! He is still writing His Story.

I guess you could say my miracle of meeting Shirley would be like "This, That and Other Miracles". I was a freshman in college, and I'd been called to preach a couple of years earlier. As I sat in Shirley's class about missions, she would write on the chalkboard and tears began running down her cheeks. Shirley could not talk about her beloved people in Brazil without getting emotional. That was the first interaction with Shirley. I began to learn and understand her heart for the people of Brazil.

Fast forward about 10 years later, my family and I found we are arriving in Brazil for the very first time. Guess who met us at the airport? Shirley and husband Jim welcomed us as we began our missionary journey.

As we lived our first months in Brazil with Jim and Shirley, we were introduced to our new life in Brazil. We came to really know and love Jim and Shirley Combs. They had been our professors and encouragers while we were in college. This couple cared deeply for many and we were no exception. I don't know if we adopted them or if they adopted us, but our children lovingly referred to them as their Brazilian grandparents. So today, with honor and pride and with tears on my own cheeks, I write this forward.

This book, like the others Shirley has written, reveals the hearts and the day-to-day activities of the Brazilian people she so dearly loves. The stories shared in this book represent life journeys of many people who Shirley committed her life to as she cared for and ministered in Brazil.

As you read "This, That, and Other Miracles", you will find God showing up on time and on purpose! He is always on purpose as He moved in the lives of His people. I still remember the first time I saw Shirley's prayer and praise list. She would roll it up and then she would unroll it to write some more scribbled notes. She documented the answered prayers and miracles the Lord was doing right in front of her each day. This book is a continuation of the prayer and praise roll she had taped together. It became a scroll filled with the responses of God! Read about how God responded and how God acted on behalf of the people Shirley Combs knew and loved.

May you fall in love with the Brazilian people through these stories just as I did, but more importantly may this book help you commit to your own prayer journey with the expectancy that God will make a difference and your own cheeks will be wet with tears.

Curt Holland
Director of Field Ministry Personnel
International Missions of Free Will Baptists
Nashville, Tennessee

The
Curt Holland
Family

PREFACE

Are you ready to be amazed and shocked by stories of God-miracles of the impossible and almost unbelievable? What I share in the following pages are miracle answers I have experienced first-hand or have met the people who excitedly showed me before and after photos of their miracle stories.

I don't know if you readers believe in modern day miracles but believing in miracles means losing your independence. Dependence on God is just another word for Power.

When I was a teenager I read Andrew Murray's book, ***With Christ in the School of Prayer***, which left an impression on me. I listened to missionaries who sat around my folks' table and told miracle answers to prayer. About 20 years ago Bruce Wilkinson wrote about praying boldly to turn the ordinary into the extraordinary.

Wilkinson wrote, "Dependence on God makes heroes of ordinary people." You can experience God working through you and you become convinced that only God could have done it. We depend totally on God in a situation, totally on His Spirit to be our sufficiency. You, the common factor, become a participant with an extraordinary God.

But beware. When Satan sees you praying for the supernatural, he will start planning to target you. To attack you and your family. But stay in the battle so that Satan will be worried about you. He fears front-line warriors. In James 4:7 it teaches "resist the devil and he will flee from you."

Depend upon God's shield, protection and supernatural powers. God may not hear this kind of prayer very often. In His model prayer he included "deliver us from evil." And when offenses come He has given us the armor needed, Ephesians 6:10. We don't need to struggle in fear of defeat. I have never seen Jesus lose a battle with the powers of darkness!

In the following stories you will meet ordinary people who received power to be His witnesses. Humbling, exhilarating, and life changing. Maybe you will be overwhelmed at how God answers courageous prayers.

It's true. Prayer works!

"My prayer is that when I die,
All of hell rejoices that
I am out of the fight!"
C.S. Lewis

Suggested Readings: For more stories on mission work in Brazil I suggest these books written by FWB missionaries.

• SHARING GOD'S GRACE
by Bobby and Geneva Poole

• AN AMAZING JOURNEY
by Bobby and Sue Aycock.

PART ONE

Months of Miracles

"That which we have seen and heard we declare unto
you, that you also may have fellowship with us…
And these things we write unto you, that your joy may
be full."
I John 1:3, 4 (KJV)

CHAPTER 1
Three Months in Brazil

The man raised his fist at us and yelled in Portuguese, *"Nao quero. E' mentira. Nao funciona!"* (I don't want that. It's a lie. It doesn't work.) What was going on? I will explain.

Usually the Friday morning street market in Araras was full of friendly greetings among neighbors and shoppers. People from the neighborhood were already selecting the fresh fruits and vegetables, dairy products, fish, straw hats, and even buttons and thread.

I arrived earlier than the Volks van full of American high school E-TEAM members, so I watched the shoppers. They placed their purchases in canvas bags or in little wire baskets on wheels used to take their purchases home. Later the bags and wire baskets would be folded until the next street market day. The street market moved from neighborhood to neighborhood on different days of the week. They would be back.

I had parked my car near the street market which was roped off for the weekly event. Before the old Volks nine-passenger van arrived that would bring the E-TEAM high school students, I walked between the booths where they displayed their wares.

The smells and chatter along the block-long market lining both sides of the street took me back to 1965 when I ventured out with my little Portuguese dictionary and handy wire cart on wheels to buy some fruits and vegetables before my afternoon session of language school study. Jim's language schedule was in the morning, so I was alone. At that time, I didn't recognize certain fruits and vegetables.

"*Gilo'?* Is that a fruit or vegetable?"

"*Chuchu? Benengela? Mamao?* If I bought them, I wouldn't know how to prepare them! I rolled my basket back to our little rented place with only a few things I recognized – potatoes, carrots, and eggs.

And the Brazilian money? Each day the exchange rate changed, and so did its value. The paper bills were different sizes and colors. I just kept handing them money until the merchant smiled and nodded his head.

I was still waiting for the Volks van with the young high school E-TEAM missionaries, so I chatted with two policemen who were eating fried pastries from the corner stand where their police car was parked. I explained that a group of American teens would be passing out invitations to an event in the Free Will Baptist Church in that neighborhood where they would be participating. The teens didn't speak Portuguese but had memorized a greeting with a smile. The two policemen just nodded and continued eating.

The teens arrived and piled out of the old van then timidly looked around at the crowd. Soon it was a precious sight to see the young people meeting the strangers and using the memorized phrase, "*Jesus te Ama,*" while Brother Peter and Sister Jane, their sponsors, kept a watchful eye. Most people politely accepted the invitations, and only a few shook their heads, no.

Jackson, one of the teens, and I were near the police car when a man passed by and was offered the invitation with scriptures of hope. He lifted his fisted hands and then with palms spread and shouted,

"I don't want it. It's a lie. It doesn't work!" Jackson didn't know what he said so he just held out his hand, smiled and said, *"Jesus te Ama."* The man stood there a few seconds, then turned and left.

Sadly, I interpreted the painful, blasphemous words of the man to my young friend holding the invitation. The man had rejected the Truth, not a lie. Faith comes by hearing – if only he had taken the invitation with the scriptures to read later, then the seed of God's Word could perhaps germinate and bring salvation.

Who will be the next person to offer the hope of salvation to him and others? Soon the E-TEAM returned to their churches, families, and sponsors in the US to report on their ministries and memories. My three months' ministry continued in Brazil to see that God's Truth is not a lie. **It really does work, and how!!** The next stories reminded us.

******

Prayer Warriors Begin – Looking for Answers

One of our three churches in that Brazilian city, *Segunda Igreja Batista Livre,* asked me to give a study on the power of prayer while I was in Araras for a three-month mission trip. That study lasted over five weeks, and we saw miracle answers to the requests we had put on a long list.

Some of my participants came from backgrounds where prayer included blood sacrifices in crossroads. A chicken is sacrificed surrounded by candles, flowers, and other fetishes. Others repeated prayers directed to idols, crawling on their knees in penitence.

Some knelt before workers seated in white asking to receive "good" spirits which turned out to be tormenting demons. They were hungry to learn more about what God teaches about prayer. A great gift to Christ followers.

When you think about it, what religion doesn't practice prayer? The Buddhists, Muslims, Baptists, Catholics, Pentecostals, Mormons, Presbyterians, Methodists? The pagans in the jungles pray to the sun, moon, stars, fire and stones. They pray to the creature instead of the Creator. Satan confuses with empty rituals, and choses mediators who used to walk this earth but were never designated by God to answer prayers, to be mediators between man and God. They don't have the power to answer in a way that is best for man.

Why doesn't Satan stop prayer? Why? He isn't worried as long as no one obeys the scripture that teaches "There is one mediator between God and man, the man Christ Jesus." I Timothy 2:5. It is a serious mistake to pray to others for protection on a trip, for health challenges, or for a good marriage for your children. God is a jealous God, and He wants to take care of His creation, but Satan has blinded many with his lies.

There is no other name under the sun with the power to answer the requests we had on our list during those weeks. Miracles can lead us to the door of faith. It gets the attention of people so that they will listen to the truth and behold the beauty of the Truth in Christ.

Now I want to share just a few of the miracle answers during those three months. **It isn't a lie. It works!!**

******

A Miracle from Europe to Brazil - Answer 1

Soon after I arrived, a lady from the Tuesday prayer study invited me to visit their home to pray for their son. He had recently been sent home from a hospital in Czechoslovakia. The young man started going to church in Araras after contact with a group of teens, E-TEAM, a few years ago. He knelt at our church altar, and his mother's tears were the first to stain our newly built unfinished altar. He even studied one semester at a Christian College in the US.

His international firm took him to Czechoslovakia where he worked many years. But he turned his back on the Lord, and his health suffered. He was rushed to the hospital where they notified his family that there was no more they could do for him. His system had shut down.

His mother told them over the phone to hold off and she would take the first plane from Brazil and settle the situation. She arrived and hardly recognized her son. The diagnosis was that there was water on the brain, he needed a lung transplant, and a kidney transplant. She was determined to take him back to her country and put his life in God's hands.

They had been back in Araras just a few day before I arrived. When I was called to their home, I saw he had lost a lot of weight, his skin was yellow, and he had to hold on to something or someone when he walked.

I asked the young man, "What do you want me to ask for you in my prayers?"

He said, "I want to live. I want to go back to church and ask forgiveness."

We immediately put his very serious health issues on our prayer list. Weekly his mother took her son to a famous hospital in the capital city of Sao Paulo.

Praise God. The first report was that he no longer had water on his brain! Then later they discovered after more prayers and tests that he didn't need a lung transplant!

We continued to pray. You can imagine how hopeful we were at that point. Another report was that he didn't need a kidney transplant!   Doctors could not explain it and were amazed.

He started gaining weight, his color was much better and the last weekend I was there, he walked into the church on his own, stood during the singing, and praised God with his church family.

"There is one all-powerful mediator between God and man!"

Prayer really works! It isn't a lie.

******

Attempted Suicide – Answer 2

During a Wednesday prayer meeting at the *Terceira Igreja Batista Livre* our pastor José shared that a mother contacted him asking for urgent prayer for her son. The son was in the hospital in a coma. His wife had recently left him, and he swallowed a powerful poison that doctors said had destroyed his organs. Professionals didn't give much hope. His mother said he was full of tubes, and the diagnosis was that he was "brain dead." Not only did we pray and put it on our list, other churches over the city also joined us in prayer.

In each service in the many churches, prayers went up for the young man. Since they didn't know the man's spiritual situation, they wanted him to come out of his coma so that someone could talk with him about his relationship with Jesus Christ. After a few days, they reported that he had awakened and called his mother's name. That didn't sound like he was brain dead to us. With that encouragement, prayers kept hitting the throne.

Another day, they reported that he woke up again, recognized friends, and talked a little with them. Then the last Sunday I was there it was announced that he would be leaving the hospital the next day. There is power in the name of Jesus!

It isn't a lie. Prayer really works!

******

Confession Relief – Answer 3

In 1991 the police brought a nine-year-old boy to our family's home one afternoon, before we started Lar Nova Vida for the needy children in Araras. The police had heard we were looking for a home to rent and open as a home for children in crisis, but they wanted us to help them right then with a solution for this child. The child's stepfather had beaten him unconscious with a water hose because he had not brought home enough money from begging in the street. He was very shy and traumatized. Kleverton was our first child at Lar Nova Vida, and since then we have sheltered and given hope to more than 300 children.

Now he is a handsome adult, who is married and has a little girl. He is a hard worker and a deacon in his church. Recently I was in Brazil and he asked to talk with me. I met with him, and we sat in my car and talked.

He said, "I have a confession to make. I really feel badly but I don't know how to correct it now."

I thought, "Oh, no. I wonder what it is."

He continued, "My pharmacy bill was high because of my little girl's illness. Then I had to put my car in the shop. I kept putting the expenses on my credit card, and all this time I have not paid my tithe. I have paid tithes since I got my first job as a kid. Now I am far behind, and I don't know how to fix it."

I reached over to take his hand. "Son, we are going to pray about this and put it on our prayer list. First, forget for the time being about all the past tithes you owe the Lord. Then, from this day forward, pay your tithes first over everything you make." He nodded in agreement. We prayed and days passed.

A few days later I received a phone call from him.

"Mom guess what! My boss gave me some overtime work, and I can pay my tithe on it!" God heard our prayers.

Later another phone call came from him, "Mom, tomorrow is a holiday, and my boss said I can work overtime. More tithes for me to give now." He was so excited to see what God was doing.

A third phone call. "Mom, a man I work with, but don't know very well, called me over to talk. He asked if I had a credit card. I told him yes and said that I was embarrassed that I used it too much. He said that he was impressed to pay off my balance. I was so surprised!"

I was happily surprised about how God supplied, but I have seen God give beautiful answers to his children's sincere prayers.

It isn't a lie. Prayer really works.
******

Rain, Rain, Come Again – Answer 4

When I arrived in Brazil for my three-month mission trip, it had not rained in five months. Since Araras is located south of the equator, June, July, and August are winter months there. During that season without rain, many people and church groups had prayed for rain.

One day our Tuesday afternoon prayer study group got really serious and said, "Let's put rain on our prayer list." They were determined. It was added to the lists and we waited, but not for long. By the end of the week they were carrying umbrellas because a great, refreshing rain covered the city. So many were happy and relieved, but none more thankful than those women who had put rain on their list. They felt they had joined with God to supply an important need for their city.

It isn't a lie. It really works.
******

American Airlines Reschedule – Answer 5

For the last few years I have been blessed to have my airline tickets to and from Brazil provided for me by a couple from our church in Albany, Georgia, Doctor Jim and Bobbie Jo Lee. They have visited Brazil over 14 times and love the ministry there, too.

The date and duration of this three-month's mission trip came as a surprise. God knew the months He wanted me there and for how long. On Wednesday, June 6, Bobbie Jo invited me to go to Brazil with her on Sunday, the 10th. I was working and had only three days to prepare, but I went right home and started to pack. I Was Going to Brazil!! She usually schedules me to stay one month, but when I received my tickets it was for three months. Yes!

The first two days we arrived in Araras Bobbie Jo went with me to deliver uniforms just in time for a championship tournament for the jiu-jitsu team, a project she and her husband had started for the children. Then she and her mother arrived the last week of my three-month visit. A few weeks before the two women arrived, the church announced that a special drama group was scheduled to perform at their church. They said they host the group each year and the church is always full, even the balcony. They wanted the three of us to attend, and I told them we would be delighted. What was the date? On Saturday, the 25th of that month, uh-oh. Our tickets were to leave on the 23rd of August, I sadly explained to Pastor Israel.

The pastor announced from the pulpit, "Folks, we have an urgent prayer request. We need to pray that American Airlines would change the return ticket dates for Dona Shirley, Bobbie Jo, and her mother, Bobbie Jean. We really want them to be here for our special service on Saturday, the 25th." This announcement was made at each church service in the following days.

Even though I was touched by their desire to have us there, I just didn't know how to approach Bobbie Jo. So I didn't. After all, she already furnishes me a free ticket each year, and it would cost her at least $100 per ticket to change the date.

It turned out that I didn't need to mention it. Our prayer warriors had already mentioned it to the Lord.

One day Bobbie Jo called saying, "We need to talk. Doc Jim came into the office to talk about our American Airline schedule. He said something needed to be changed about the return dates. So, instead of the return date on the 23rd he thought we should place it on the 27th. Does that sound okay with you, Shirley?"

As she was explaining, I began to smile and then chuckled, "Bobbie Jo, there is a group of people down here praying that the American Airline schedule would be changed so that we could attend a special service, but I just didn't have a good way to tell you. This had to be a God thing. They will be happy to hear about this answer to prayer."

Now she was chuckling. I continued, "But I am so sorry you had to spend the extra money to change the dates."

"Oh, no. They didn't charge us anything." Sounded like another God thing to me.

The two women arrived, and we attended a delightful presentation of the Gospel by the drama team and were able to witness a full house in attendance. At the dismissal, the pastor asked me to go to the front for the closing prayer. He told the audience that God changed American Airlines scheduled just for all of us that night.

The congregation burst out with clapping and cheering – for God!

It is not a lie. Prayer really does work.
****

A Bus Ride with a Purpose – Answer 6

About two weeks before ending my three months in Brazil, I received an invitation to one of our churches from Renata Poole in Ribeirao Preto. That would mean a bus ride of about two hours. Besides visiting the Sunday services, I was asked to speak to their women about prayer on the following Tuesday.

I had taken the bus on Saturday to spend the weekend with the family of a deacon of that church, the Ferreiras. They are the Brazilian in-laws of my daughter Tania. I thought about the talk with the women, all of whom were active, dedicated women who meet regularly. Father, what do you want to say to them?

Thoughts came - Remind them of the power in the name and blood of Jesus. Tell them of the times demons fled at that name. Remind them that they can see the power if they use that name.

Okay. But Satan is not going to like it!

Tuesday came, and I saw a room full of probably 20 beautiful ladies. When they introduced me for the lesson, they all sat down in a semi-circle, and I was seated in front of them.

I chose to share personal experiences from the last 54 years of seeing God win over the powers of darkness. For God's glory, I will share them with you now. You, too, will find out why God chose that message.

****

Legion

One Sunday night during an evangelist campaign at the *Igreja Batista Livre* in Araras, we had several visitors our new members had invited. One of these visitors, invited by a friend, was a small lady sitting at the end of a pew. Suddenly during the sermon, the lady fell over into the aisle.

Since at that time it was not unusual to see a manifestation of demons during preaching or prayer, the deacons and congregation knew what to do. When a human body is possessed by demons, for some reason it is very heavy. So even though she was a small woman, several men gathered around her, lifted her, and carried her into a small Sunday School room in the back corner of the church.

The congregation automatically started singing songs about the blood and name of Jesus. They knew there was a spiritual battle going on in that Sunday School room. They sang *"Foi Na Cruz"* (At the Cross), and *"Ha' Poder no Sangue de Jesus"* (There is Power in the Blood).

In the little room the woman was in a trance, sitting in a wooden chair with her head resting on her chin. We were sitting against the wall praying in the powerful name of Jesus and claiming His blood over the situation. We knew the demons could hear us, and they weren't giving up easily. The battle continued.

A demon spoke in a low growl through the vocal cords of the woman. "We won't leave her. She is too good for us."

The evangelist asked, "How long has she been possessed?"

The voice answered, "Three months."

"What is your name?" he asked the demon.

"My name is *legiao* because we are many," it answered.

Wow. Just like in the Bible. Its name was Legion. The poor lady must have suffered so much, but that was about to change. The powerful name of Jesus will liberate and set free. We must keep praying and singing about the blood.

Scripture was preached about the sovereignty of God. About the glorious story of the cross and resurrection of Jesus Christ. About the power in the blood. We sang. Prayed. The demons resisted and jerked the woman around.

Suddenly she lifted her head, eyes closed, and turned it slowly toward the door. She opened her eyes, "He is gone now. He is gone."

Sweet victory. We talked to the woman and explained what God had done and that now that she was rid of the evil spirit, she must accept the Holy Spirit into her life. She accepted with a grateful smile and happy tears.

She said she felt light and whole. No more sights of hideous spirits tormenting her in her home at night. No more pain and depression that she thought would drive her crazy. She was free. She was not alone. Sweet victory.

****

We will kill him!

A lady from our church was concerned about her son who did not attend with her. Before she accepted

Christ, she was a Spiritist medium and became a Christ follower after her children were grown.

One afternoon we arrived at her house, and she led us into her living room. I sat on her long sofa with others. As soon as we were settled we heard strange, and loud laughing from another room. Cackling laughter. One colleague with us whispered that it sounded like the demon of laughter along with the demon of blasphemy. It was all still new to me, and I didn't even know they had names.

We opened our Portuguese Bibles while the lady went into the bedroom to call her son. We use a scripture in I John 1:7 in these situations to hopefully convince the person to read it aloud. Why? The end of the verse has these words "…and the **blood** of **Jesus Christ** cleanses us of all sin." The ones who refuses to read it, or who chokes up and is unable to read it usually ends up having a demonic manifestation. The evil spirits know the power of that name.

Finally, the son came out of the bedroom and greeted us politely in the living room. He went around shaking our hands, asking polite questions about our families or activities. So normal. He sat down to my left on the sofa.

We started reading scriptures, and I shared my Bible with him. I read verse six so it was his turn to read verse seven. I felt everyone was breathing a prayer just as I was. He started reading the verse, "But if we walk in the light as He is…" He passed my Bible back to me. He complained of his throat and said that someone else should read. Several urged him to continue reading.

He reluctantly took my Bible again to read. As he started to read the part of the verse that says "…and the **blood of Jesus Christ,"** he started coughing and choking and slid off the sofa onto the floor in front of me. His body began to jerk, and he started making growling sounds and doing something I have never seen in other cases - foaming at the mouth. Sounds like a Biblical story.

From his own vocal cords came a low voice, *"Nao cante Foi Na Cruz"*. (Don't sing At the Cross.)

"Nao cante, senao eu mato ele." (Don't sing or I will kill him.)

Guess what we did? We all started singing, *"Foi na Cruz, Foi na Cruz."* The demon put up a fight, and his body went into convulsions for a few seconds, then went limp, face down.

The men helped him up onto the sofa again. He was exhausted. They explained the story of the gospel and the need for salvation in Jesus Christ. They told him that now that he was free of the bad spirits, he needed to invite the Holy Spirit into his life.

"Maybe another day," he said. "I am tired now. I don't want to pray about it now. Maybe another day."

They explained what the Bible says about spirits leaving and that more will return after the "house" has been swept clean. He still didn't want to listen and said maybe he would consider it on another day.

He never accepted the Lord and his mother said that it seems the evil spirits had returned worse than ever!

******

I'll Ruin Him Financially

One Sunday our family was sitting around the table having finished lunch after church when I answered a phone call. That was not unusual, nor was the request from the caller.

Our foster son, Marco Antonio, asked, "Sorry to bother you, but I need you to go to Antonio and Sandra's house across from the church to help me pray for them." He set a time to meet there.

I agreed, and the family said to go ahead. As I pulled off my apron, I started praying. I usually like to be fasting before these cases, but since I didn't know beforehand and had just eaten lunch, I felt that God's power wasn't limited to anything I did or did not do. So I reached for the car keys and left to face the battle that Christ had already won.

When I arrived at their house, Marco was already talking to the family, the husband, wife, adult son, and an adolescent son. They received me with the usual kisses on the checks and hugs then we all sat down.

Marco explained the salvation gospel to the spiritually hungry group. Then he turned to *Señor* Antonio, the husband, and asked him to stand. He asked me to stand behind the man. Sometimes people in a trance sway back and forth and fall backward.

He said, "I am going to pray, and you might go into a trance. Then I will speak to what manifests itself. Perhaps I will speak harshly to it, but I won't be speaking to you. Do you understand?"

"Sim, Senhor."

Marco began to pray, and Senhor Antonio's chin dropped to his chest with his eyes closed. The battle began. We prayed in the name of Jesus and declared the power of His blood. We prayed and sang. The evil spirit finally spoke through the vocal cords of the poor man in the trance.

"I will not leave him. I will ruin him financially."

Marco told the demon that he had no authority over the life of a man who was reaching out to God, who desired to be free through Jesus Christ. Antonio began clinching his fist and swaying back and forth.

Marco raised his voice at the demon and said, "Stop swaying back and forth. You are not going to throw this man on the floor!"

Senhor Antonio's body quit swaying, but his fists were still clinched. After more moments of using the name and blood of Jesus, the man jerked and then went limp. He was quickly caught and taken to a chair, exhausted.

Marco dealt in the same way with the wife and adolescent son but there was no manifestation. But with the adult son, there was.

Marco asked him to stand and asked me to stand behind him. Prayers. Songs about the blood. He also fell into a trance.

A spirit manifested in him and said the same words, "I will ruin him financially." Finally, that spirit left, too, and he was helped to a chair.

While we were all seated and somewhat exhausted, Marco looked around at each of us and spoke to the family.

"The other day after we spoke you gathered up your idols and images and gave them to me.

Can you think of anything left here that would give Satan the idea that he had a right to invade your house again?"

The wife and adult son left their seats and went into their bedrooms. They both returned with something in the palm of their hands. One was a small plastic crucifix on a chain and the other was a small crucifix and chain that looked to be some type of metal. Marco leaned forward and placed his elbows on his knees, looking into their eyes, holding the items in his hands.

He said quietly, "These are symbols that are very precious to you since they represent the terrible sacrifice Jesus paid for our salvation."

The family nodded in agreement.

"But what if Satan wanted to design an icon/symbol of his day of victory over Jesus Christ. What do you think he would design?'

They looked at the items in their hands. A dead Christ. I had never thought of that.

"To us the empty cross reminds us of God's victory over Satan and death. What would you like to do with those things?"

Both quickly gave them to Marco. He handed them to me and asked me to do away with them. That wasn't a problem since I had destroyed others before. But it would soon be time to go to the evening service, and now I had some items to destroy.

I said my goodbyes with the same cheek kisses and hugs and quickly got in my car to drive home. I drove my car through the open gate at home and stopped close to the front porch. Before going into the house, I started making a small hole in the front yard. I put some twigs and pieces of paper into the hole and dropped in the two items. After going into the house for matches, I started a fire, and it began to consume the items.

It is always a serious moment for me since I felt an act like that would not be pleasing to Satan. So I started singing *"Ha Poder No Sangue de Jesus"* (There is Power in the Blood). The neighbors walking by may have thought *'Americana louca'* seeing me looking down at some tiny smoke and singing to myself!

I kicked dirt over the little fire after the items had melted. I quickly ran into the house to prepare to return to the church, since flip- flops didn't match my skirt!

When I arrived at the church, the service had already begun. As I walked through the back door, I saw on the last row their four beaming faces smiling at me and singing. What were they singing?

"There is power, power, wonder working power

In the blood of the lamb!" Amen. Yes, sweet victory.

****

On the Bus Again

Now I take you back to the women at the Ribeirao Preto church. After sharing the above stories with the women, we all stood together. I had delivered the message, but was God finished? As we sang together before dismissing, there was a commotion and several of the women huddled together looking down. I stayed in my place and started praying. The women were praying, too.

On the floor lay one of the young women. Caring friends were around her declaring the name and blood of

Jesus. Now I understood the message God had chosen. The women knew they had heard, seen, and felt something from the victorious Christ.

It was time to catch the bus back to the city of Araras so I needed to leave. While waiting for the bus to depart, I was reminded of the wisdom and power of God. He had plans for the ladies' meeting, and I was privileged to be a part of it. Thank you, Father.

A young man sat in the seat beside me. One more person to share the Good News with.

It's not a lie. It really works!

Chapter 2
Our Quiver Full of Arrows

At 17 my husband shot his first deer in West Virginia with a bow and arrow, and he liked to tell the story. I am sure his folks were proud that he could add meat to their freezer as their other sons had done. And they ended up with nine sons and six daughters. Yes, 15 children.

Perhaps that is why Jim liked to quote the scripture: "Children are a heritage from the Lord, like arrows in the hand of a warrior… Happy is the man who has his quiver fill of them." We had no idea that God had a plan to full our quiver with more than 300 street children.

In my other books I described how the city government asked our young *Igreja Batista Livre* in Araras, Sao Paulo, Brazil, to open a home for children in crisis. We asked for three months to get together a plan and to see if that is what God had for us as a part of the community. Sorry, but a question did cross my mind whether we had gone to Brazil to be "social workers?"

But during that time the police started bringing children at risk to our private home. And we were filled with love, God's love for these children. We soon discovered that, yes, the city did need a home for street children. These children the police brought to our home had been abused, used, abandoned, and were caught up in a cycle. Also, the children needed a group to provide a shelter/home as a family, giving hope and Christian values to these precious children. And they would need a house mother, food, furniture, medical care, schooling, and acceptance. We had none of these things, and the city government had only promised to rent one home. Best of all, we had a loving Heavenly Father, and if He is opening the door, then we will walk through it.

So, we started a prayer list! That was in 1991. Now that prayer list is a two-sided, nine-foot list of ANSWERED prayers.

When we went to the scriptures, we kept reading in Psalms: "Defend the poor and fatherless. Do justice to the affected and needy. Free them from the hand of the wicked. They do not know, nor do they understand. They walk in darkness."

"God is a father of the fatherless, a defender of widows."

"God sets the solitary in families."

Wow! How can you ignore the message? So, Lar Nova Vida, New Life Children's Home was born.

****

Empty Houses. Who moved the children?

At first it was difficult to find people who would rent to Lar Nova Vida. They would say, "My house to put street children in? No way!"

But during the next few years we rented six houses. Usually they would only rent to us for a year at a time, and then we would have to move again. The law required no more than 10 children per house mother. We kept renting houses as our Lar Nova Vida family kept growing, but the city government would only rent one house as per the original agreement.

Finally, after God worked His amazing miracles we moved into our own two beautiful homes and other buildings. Five bedrooms, three baths in each home. At one time the judge sent up to 20 children per house.

After 44 years as resident missionaries in Brazil, God allowed my husband and me to move to Oklahoma to be near our Brazilian-born children and grandchildren (all have dual citizenship).

Because of a generous FWB couple in Georgia, we were able to return each year and spend time with and serve our beloved churches and children's homes. On each trip we were able to bring offerings to help the churches and children's homes.

On one visit when I came with an offering to help replace doors, buy paint, check minor plumbing and electrical needs, I found the houses were empty! The city had forced LNV to move and to rent a house near downtown. The houses were empty. The children were gone.

When I asked for an explanation, I was told that the city government sent word that we would NEVER return to our houses. Our houses that love built. Our own team of workers and professionals said that there was no need to spend money to fix up our own houses. They said I was just wasting time and money.

I remembered the story of Nehemiah who was trying to rebuild walls. While people tried to discourage him, he just kept on working as God had planned for him to do. God had worked miracles to acquire the land, and to build and open up the homes for the redemption of needy children. So I just kept on working, too, with the help of volunteers. Lots of volunteers.

When my weeks were up and I needed to return to my home in Oklahoma, the houses were beautiful. Fresh. Renewed. Beautiful furnishings. But still empty! As my plane left Brazil I prayed for our children, their families, our workers, and the city government. When God was ready, two beautiful houses stood ready to receive our children once again.

And guess what? On my return visit to Araras a year later, our children had been returned to our homes, and I finally found the houses filled with happy, healthy children. God answers prayers.

Quiver Explosions!

During the three months I was in Brazil, the Catholic nuns closed their shelter for girls, and the authorities turned the girls over to us. We opened the third house in the city of Araras for girls. That same year two other cities asked us to open a Lar Nova Vida Children's Homes to serve their communities. They said they would take care of the finances if we would manage them. We opened the fourth and fifth Lar Nova Vida.

One year later two more cities asked to open Lar Nova Vida for their communities. They would take care of the finances and asked us to manage them. That meant we could send Christian house parents, psychologists, social workers, and other helpers to care for precious children in need. To give hope and health to many others.

From the declaration that our homes would NEVER open again to now operating seven homes for the glory of

God and the redemption of needy children, we can say that we are awed by God's foresight.

Courage to persevere in the will of God in ministry is important. We had seven quivers full. God answers prayers.

******

Surprise by Snail-mail

Most of the payer partners and sponsors of Lar Nova Vida don't speak Portuguese or couldn't afford passports, visas, and airplane tickets to go visit them in Brazil.

So, I want to tell you how some of these special friends were present for an event in Brazil without taking a flight or speaking Portuguese. And they didn't even know about the need they were going to help meet.

In November four of us met in Araras to serve our churches and the Lar Nova Vida New Life Children's Home. Bobbie Jo from Georgia, her mother Bobbie Jean from Florida, and my daughter Cindy and I from Oklahoma, traveled to Brazil. The four of us represented friends who sent us with their blessings, offerings, and prayers.

Johnny, one of our Brazilian spiritual sons, met us in the Sao Paulo International Airport and took us and our many bags to Araras. We were to spend a few weeks serving in the ministry anyway we could.

The promised monthly small government grant had not been given for five months to the Children's Home. The day the check arrived for them with the back pay, it was blocked at the bank. We had heard of the urgent needs of the Children's Home, received offerings, and made a priority list.

    - to buy fruits and vegetables
    - to buy a used refrigerator
    - two used four burner stoves
    - a large table with 10 chairs
    - a used washing machine
    - three chest of drawers (six drawers)
    - food for the freezer.

We also wanted to pay some of their bills. Each year we try to host a party of hot dogs and ice cream in the park for all the children, the workers and their children

On the first day we arrived we saw the nine passenger Volks van in a sad, sad shape. The passenger sliding door was wired shut.

I asked, "Why is it wired like that?"

"Well, when we drive down the street, the door falls off into the street. We have had it repaired, but it still doesn't stay on. It is dangerous for the children, so we wire it."

I looked through the window and saw that the middle bench had fallen.

"Why doesn't someone fix that bench?" I asked without trying to sound critical,

"Okay, if you look at the floorboard, you will see that it is too rusty to hold the bolts that fasten the bench. When it is full of children, it doesn't fall over. We have tried to repair it many times. It makes it difficult to use the seat belts."

Shocking situation. Johnny whispered to me that we must find a better transportation for the children. I agreed, but how? They needed food, and the pharmacy and gas bills also needed to be paid.

November is summertime in Brazil, so we stood with the hot sun on our head looking at the sad Volks van.

Johnny offered to look for a used van in better shape. In fact, he said it had to be a priority. He said he thought he could find one for the equivalent of $3,000, and maybe we could find enough people to raise that much.

I looked at his sincere interest. "But I am leaving in three weeks. I know that we want this and need this, but we need to put our knees to the floor and see what God thinks we need to do."

In three weeks, we had raised most of the three thousand American dollars, thanks to help from the American friends who came with us. But Johnny had not found a van for that price. When he did find one in the third week, it was double the price.

It was much better than we hoped for, but double the price? Others were consulted, and most of them said it was in an excellent shape and was worth much more than the asking price.

Lar Nova Vida's budget is based on "save it before you buy it," and this practice has served us well for many years. However, this amount would have to be paid the next week. A friend and businessman in town heard about the situation and offered to loan us the second half. He said we could pay it back in payments as offerings came in.

There was nothing in Lar Nova Vida's budget to contribute. What the friend who offered to loan the money didn't know was that we had only a few small offerings from US Free Will Baptists: an offering from a church in

Georgia, an offering from a couple in West Virginia, and three offerings from Oklahoma. It would take years to pay back $3,000!

Oh, how I needed to talk to the Lord about this.

"Father, I confess that LNV needs a better, safer transportation, and they also need food, medicines, and money to pay bills and the workers. It would take years to pay back the loan.

"I confess that I pictured myself going door to door begging help to pay off this loan. I have never had to do that, and I don't want to do that. But am I being prideful? Am I not listening to the Brazilian workers here who think it is a good buy and should be done? I want to respect their opinions. We have always saved first, then bought. You have always come through on the plan. I have written three books full of reminders to others and to myself of just what a faithful Father you are to the orphans and widows."

"Please, Father, let me see your heart in this."

Two of our mission team members had already left, and soon my daughter Cindy and I would be leaving. The date for deciding on the van was arriving, too. A scripture from Psalms 62 came to my mind. Is there something in there for us?

> "My soul, wait silently for God alone,
> For my expectation is from Him.
> He only is my rock and my salvation;
> Trust in Him at all times,
> Pour out your heart before Him;
> God is a refuge for us."

Hey, I was talking to my Father who had helped our Brazilian Christian teams to shelter and plant seeds of hope in the lives of over 300 children in the last almost 30 years. Many of those children came from begging in the streets to now becoming citizens giving back to the community, and some are in the ministry. His faithfulness had already filled the three books I had written. Okay, was that a green light?

The day came for my daughter and me to catch our flight back to Oklahoma, and we still had not made a decision about the van. On the way to the airport I kept meditating on the words "wait silently for God alone" and 'my expectation is from Him" and 'trust in Him at all times." Peace. A big, silent "YES' came to me. "God alone." Okay. Let's do it!

As soon as we checked in at the American Airlines counter, I said to Cindy, "Call the guys. The deal is a go." She immediately got on the phone, and they put things in motion to close the deal the next day. I chuckled to myself. Maybe I would enjoy going from door to door asking for help. I just knew I would wait upon the Lord. The night before we had seen a teen from the children's home being baptized. That was what it was all about. They will have a safe vehicle. I left with a happy heart, ready to see how God was going to handle one more miracle.

We arrived at the Oklahoma City Will Rogers International Airport and then home safely. I wheeled my luggage into my bedroom and breathed, "Home Sweet Home." My son, Kemper, had put my three months of mail on the middle of my king-size bed. I forgot about unpacking and started opening the pile of letters.

Many addresses I didn't even recognize. To my surprise, they held checks. Checks for Lar Nova Vida. I opened the ones with addresses I recognized. More checks.

These dates were from before we were even debating and praying about a van. God knew His plans, but the people didn't know the need when they decided to participate in the ministry.

I punched in my phone calculator to add up the checks' values. Can you guess how much the total was? $3,000! Yes. I was awed by God's foresight, His omniscience. He is my Father, and He loves needy little children and those who take care of them. He is a Father to the orphan and a husband to the widows.

Immediately I called Cindy to advise those in Brazil that we already had the money to pay off the loan. That meant that it would be paid for before it was delivered. Did we "save it first and then buy it?" We had it. We had the amount necessary to pay off the loan before the Volks van Kombi was delivered. Debt free. God and American friends partnered and supplied the need before the deal even came up.

It took a while to deliver, register, transfer documents, and complete all other paperwork needed for a vehicle donated to a non-profit organization. Then I received word that they were going to have a ceremony to present the keys. They did it up Brazilian style.

So the month before Christmas in summer-time Brazil in the main park in downtown Araras, Sao Paulo, before many witnesses, the keys and title of a beautiful white Volks van Kombi were presented to the board and president of Lar Nova Vida.

Across one side of the Volks Van was stretched a banner:

(Translation)
"This vehicle is an offering of love in memory of
Missionary James Kemper Combs,
A memorial on the altar of Jesus Christ."
Without needing to send folks on jet planes with passports
to Brazil, before we had even closed the deal, God had sent
His Christmas miracle surprise by US snail-mail.

What an adventure to put faith and trust in our
Father God!

(About a year after that dedication, the city
government of Araras named a local park after Pastor
Jaime Combs.)

******

Chapter 3
My Name Is………..

Recently I read an article in the *"RENEW Magazine"* about one's name. We can know our name, who we are, and embrace that. There are identities we start at birth. After each comma there is another phase. We are someone's male child or female child, maybe someone's sister or brother, someone's cousin, someone's playmate, neighbor, classmate, roommate, employee, employer, someone's partner, someone's parent, someone's grandparent, someone's mentor. All of the people involved in these stages have become part of the meaning of our name.

Then there are titles. I have been called preacher's kid, speaker, teacher, secretary-bookkeeper, author, missionary, and the most important title is a child of God.

One Wednesday night when I was nine years old I made the most important decision of my life. My pastor father had invited a young preacher for a revival, L. A. Yandell, and I guess I paid more attention those nights. On Wednesday night my baby sister Carolyn and I went forward and knelt at the altar accepting Christ as Savior and "boss" of our lives. The two of us and our older brother Wayne were soon baptized in a creek in Berryhill, Oklahoma.

The Lord put a desire in my heart to share that wonderful experience with others, and I have had many opportunities to do so. But since then, only three persons have approached me personally and witnessed to me.

The First

The first person who ever witnessed to me personally saw me in the church parking lot after Sunday morning service when I was about nine years old. I was crying and a church pillar Buck Woolsey saw me and asked me if I was crying because I wanted to "ask Jesus into my heart."

I said, "No, I want to go home with Margie and Mother won't let me." But that question stayed with me, and soon I did "ask Jesus into my heart."

******

The Second

The second person who witnessed to me was in the Amazon jungle. After a five-year term as missionaries in Brazil, we remembered a special invitation we had received during our first year there in language school in 1965. Sandra Cue was a linguist missionary in a refresher language course with others from her New Tribes Mission. Soon there was a special connection between us. On our way to our first stateside assignment, we flew to a simple airport in northern Brazil in the *Territorio de Roraima* to visit them.

There Eldon Larson, a pilot with Missionary Aviation Fellowship (*Asas de Socorro),* flew us and our children Kemper and Cindy to spend ten unforgettable days in the Amazon jungle. Unforgettable also was the ride through those mountains and the Amazon jungle that left me green with sickness. I held on because I knew we were facing the opportunity of a lifetime.

Our tiny plane was met by primitive Indians. Naked. No clothes, but they wore flowers and sticks through pierced ear and noses. They gave us a curious, hands-on welcome, and they asked a surprising question.

As we were surrounded by naked Indians, the men would beat one hand on their chest repeating a phrase. Their language was unknown to the civilized world, and Sandra and her team were registering it for the first time.

They beat their chest and repeated what sounded like, "*Djedjustwabutu*".

I turned to missionary Sandra and asked, "What are they saying? Asking?"

She answered with a smile, "They are asking if Jesus lives in your chest."

Wow! Glory! A naked Indian in the Amazon jungle just witnessed to me. Their language was recorded, the Word was translated and taught, and now God lives in their chests. They shared that Good News with me. I was an adult, married with two children, before the second person witnessed personally to me. Thank you, Mr. Indian. Yes, I have Jesus in my chest. Thank you for asking.

****

The Third

By the third time someone personally witnessed to me, my three children had already finished college and had families of their own. Jim and I were waiting in the island capital of the state of *Santa Catarina* to catch a plane. The airport was right on the beach in *Florianopolis,* and we arrived early so we took a walk on the beach with friends from the city of *Tubarao (*Shark City.*)* They had driven us to the airport and waited with us for departure time.

It was Easter weekend. There were many people on the beach and others fishing from the pier. From one group of young people we heard instruments, singing and laughter. We couldn't read the sign they were carrying until they started toward us.

They approached us all smiles and greeted us in Portuguese with, "Happy Easter. We are here celebrating that God's Son Jesus is alive today after dying on the cross for our sins. He is in heaven now preparing a place for all who believe in Him as Savior. Do you know the story?"

Smiling, I said, "Yes, I do."

They continued in Portuguese, "Did you know that you can have the living Jesus in your heart?"

I was loving this. "Yes, I know that."

"Then would you like to accept Him as Savior? Do you already have Jesus in your heart?"

There it was. "*Sim, tenho Jesus no meu coracao.*" (Yes, I have Jesus in my heart.)

I looked around at those serious, young faces. "And thank you for honoring me with that important question. Continue to invite others to know that same story. God is very happy with you. Happy Easter."

As our airplane from the *Airlines Azul* lifted off headed back to Sao Paulo, my heart was happy, too."

******

Two Minute Message

Evangelism. Friendship evangelism works for me. You show and live the Gospel before you get a chance to really share scriptures. They are more likely to listen to you then.

But what about situations when you have a short time. Maybe two minutes? What are the most important words someone needs to hear? Every sentence needs a subject, verb, and object. Some form of the verb "love" is mentioned over 600 times in the Bible. A very good verb. "God" is certainly a worthy subject and the object "you" is very personal.

So, I have some two-minute contacts. At the market checkout most attendants have name tags. The same is true at restaurants. Most people don't seem to mind if you mention their name, especially if they are wearing it for you to see. I can sincerely use certain phrases in my two minutes. God loves each person.

First, I mention their name and let them comment. I use openers such as: "You have a pretty name. Did your mother name you or did your father give you that name?" (That often opens a comment about family history.)

"Oh, your name is __. That is a Bible name." (Many times, they mention their siblings who have Bible names, too.)

"Your name reminds me of an Italian name." (or Hispanic, or other. I mention that my grandchildren have foreign names.)

Next, I usually say, "I don't know if someone has told you today that God loves you. I didn't know your name, but He does. He loves you and wants to be a part of your life."

The usual reaction is a "thank you." But sometimes tears come to the person's eye. Male or female may share that they work two jobs and really needed to hear that. Or they may say they have been away from their job for surgery and appreciated hearing that God knows them.

Once Jim and I went to a restaurant with other couples. Three of us were celebrating January birthdays. At the end of the meal, I called the waitress by name and thanked her for her good service. I mentioned her name, very popular in Brazil, and said, "I don't know if someone has told you today that God loves you. I didn't know your name, but God does, and He wants to be a part of your life." She thanked me, and we left our table.

As we were leaving the restaurant, a young waiter called after us, "Are you the lady who talked to a waitress just now?" I answered that I was. "She is crying and asked to talk to you again."

Jim and the other couples, the Deeds, the Brashiers, and the Berglans, waited for me near the door.

I went into a little service area where the crying young lady was waiting. She hugged me and told me her story. She really needed to know that someone cared and had positive plans for her.

From there the Holy Spirit had to take over again. What did she need to hear? I prayed for her and told about the love of the Lord and the plans He had to save her and take her to live with Him some day. Her tears turned into a weak smile and a hug and we said good-bye. Yes, God knew her name. God loves her.

******

Another time in a restaurant in West Virginia, the Combs relatives had gathered to visit with us over breakfast as we traveled through their state. We were home on stateside assignment with our mission, and since Jim was the third of fifteen children, it took time to see everyone before going back to Brazil.

As typical of a family gathering, there were jokes, retelling old stories, wide-eyed children, sharing recipes, health reports, and always a little music. Yes, all in the restaurant with smiling waitresses.

As we were about to leave, I looked up at one main waitress, called her by the name on here tag, and thanked her for serving us well.

I asked, "You have a beautiful Bible name. Do you know who named you?"

She smiled and touched her name tag, "They named me after my paternal grandmother."

"Well, I don't know if someone has told you today that God loves you. I didn't know your name before, but God does know your name and He knows where you are today and what you are going through. He wants to be a part of your life."

I noticed she turned around, so I stood up and touched her shoulder. She turned to me with tears in her eyes.

"You don't know how much that helped me. My grandmother just died, and I have felt so empty and alone. I haven't even looked to God to try to get through this, but He was already here. Thank you for reminding me."

Powerful words. Yes, God knows her name. God loves her.

A Stinky Hug

Two of our teens from our Brazilian children's home, *Lar Nova Vida,* were with me downtown. We were getting into my car on our way to the barber shop when a young man approached Luciano.

Some of our children had been in similar situations when they were young, begging in the streets for their relatives, before being rescued by Lar Nova Vida. The man was asking the boys for a Brazilian *Real, a* coin worth about a quarter at that time.

Each day I asked that God give me an opportunity to witness to someone. Sometimes it would be a beggar, but usually I didn't give money to beggars. We had a flexible rule about that. If they asked money for food, I would buy them a snack. If they asked money for medicine, I would take their prescription to the pharmacy. If they came to me, I gave them an opportunity to talk, then I could talk to them.

The driver side car door was still open, and I felt the "urge" to get out and talk to the man. The boys entered the car but listened through the open windows. I called out to the man and got out of the car.

He was tall and thin with wrinkled but clean clothes. Tall for the average Brazilian man and maybe in his twenties. He didn't ask me for money.

I asked him his name and if he was from Araras. I asked about his family and his situation. I said, "I didn't know your name, but God does. He wants to help you and be part of your life. He loves you. That why He sacrificed His Son so that you can have forgiveness and a new life. He loves you. Do you know who Jesus is?"

He looked at me, leaned his head to one side and tears started forming in his eyes. He surprised me by reciting, in Portuguese. Psalms 23. Every verse.

When he finished, he asked, "*Senhora,* can you give me a hug?"

I looked around and said, "*Senhor,* I think if Jesus were here he would give you a hug so I will give you a hug in Jesus' name. "

"But, *Senhora,* I am too stinky." I had noticed he didn't smell of alcohol or tobacco, but of one who had walked in the sun for many hours.

I thought for a few seconds, "Well, I still think Jesus would hug you if He were here."

After the hug I asked, "Do you know that Jesus is that Shepherd from the Psalms 23 that you quoted? He is the Son of God and is preparing a place for all the people who accept salvation through Him, and only Him."

He seemed to be listening seriously.

"You must believe that he died on the cross as a perfect sacrifice for our sins and that He is alive today. He knows you and loves you and wants to help you. But you have to invite Him."

Just then a man passed us on the sidewalk, stopped and said,

"He is a good young man, *Senhora.*" And left.

Uh, oh. There was another hug coming.

I thought, "Okay, Lord, here comes another stinky hug. If you can die for his sins, I can hug him in Your name. Use this grandmother's arms for Your glory."

Before I returned to my car, I felt a piece of paper in my jacket pocket. It was worth about four quarters in

American money. I was about to break my rule. He had not asked me for money, but as I handed the money to the young man I said,

"I can't guarantee that you will use this money for what is good for your health. It isn't much. I just have to trust you. But I will give this to you in Jesus' name. Remember what I told you and remember that Jesus loves you."

When I got back into the car my teens were all smiles. I guess they thought the delay was worth it. I think Jesus thought so, too.

******

A Dollar's Worth

Midweek prayer meetings in Brazil meet at 8:00 pm, and I was on my way early. The evening sun had set at 6:27 pm and it was dark. I drove my little Fiat to the *Terceira Igreja Batista Livre* (Third Free Will Baptist Church) situated in the Marabá neighborhood. As I drove toward the church I checked the time and realized that the church probably wouldn't be open that early. And it was too cold to wait in the car.

Each day I ask the Lord to lead me to someone to share His love. That day I had not encountered "someone." Suddenly I had an urge to turn around. Okay, but where? There was a small traffic circle in front of the Nestle Company, so I started back on the road I had just traveled.

I couldn't remember anything about that particular section, but I had been gone for a year. I saw lights up ahead. It was a new gas station on my right. Following the urge again, I quickly turned into the station and parked near a table where four men were seated.

Was I supposed to buy something? My tank was full. What is my excuse for being there? In Brazil they are truly Service Stations. They serve you by not only filling you tank for you, but they wash your windshields, check your water and oil, and ask if you want your tires checked.

Maybe I could order *café' com leite,* but they didn't have coffee with milk. As I sat in my car I remembered a young man named Ulson who used to service our personal cars at another service station. He also serviced the vehicles of Lar Nova Vida Children's Home for about 15 years. That station was now closed, and I heard that Ulson had gone to a new station to work. Could it be that he is here? Would he be working this late in the evening?

I got out of my car and looked around. The men at the table just nodded their heads politely. I saw two men at the pumps. One was an Asian gentleman, so I knew he was not my friend. The other man turned around and I recognized him. It was Ulson.

He saw me and called out, "*Dona* Shirley!" He was still holding the gas hose so I approached him so he could continue to work.

He said, "Oh, I just heard recently about *Senhor* Jaime (my late husband Jim). I was shocked when Ze' Carlos told me he had died of cancer. Such a strong man, and always friendly."

He finished at the pump, reached out, and surprised me with a hug. He was grieving, and maybe it was what he was needing. He opened his wallet and showed me an American one-dollar bill.

"*Senhor* Jaime gave this to me years ago as a souvenir. I have kept it all this time." Then he showed me several other one dollar bills he had gotten from Jim over the years.

I reached into my purse and passed over the Brazilian *Reais* bills and found an American dollar bill to add to his collection. I needed to talk to him before another customer pulled up to a pump.

"Ulson," I started in Portuguese, "Jaime is alive and free of sickness in heaven. God loved us so much that He sent His only Son to die in our place and is alive to prepare a place for us. We have to believe and accept. And we can meet Jim again when God calls us. Jim will be waiting for us. God loves you, Ulson, and wants to be a part of your life."

It was a special moment for both of us, but he needed to return to work, and it was time for me to go to church. He hugged me again and offered to help me in any way he could.

As I drove back to our little church, I had a smile on my face.

Okay, Lord, I got my dollars' worth tonight.

******

Bus Trip With Mr. Famous X

I was boarding a *Viasol* bus back to Araras after speaking at a women's meeting in the city of Ribeiro Preto. Part of traveling by air or by bus is the opportunity the Lord opens for me to meet interesting people. I asked to be used as I laid my head against the back of the seat and looked out the bus window. It had been a busy weekend, and an intense meeting, so I was glad to rest for a few minutes and think about all that God had done that very day.

What? Looking out the window I saw a lady in Bermuda shorts, a T-shirt, and a ball cap covering her short-bleached haircut. She looked familiar, but I thought that lady was dead or still in jail. In fact, she went to prison for killing a man in that very bus station. I had been rearing her three children since they were in diapers and here she was. Lord, is she the one I am supposed to speak to? I wanted to talk to her and watched as she crossed the station carrying a duffle bag. She entered the *Rapido do Oesto* bus to the city of *Pocos de Caldas*. Before I could decide if I should leave my bus to try to talk to her, her bus left.

My bus was about to leave and the seat next to me was still empty. Well, maybe I could rest a little since the Lord hadn't sent someone. Woops. A young man entered the bus and took his seat next to mine. As soon as he sat down he took out a book by an American author translated into Portuguese. It was a book about online trading, so I thought I shouldn't bother him just yet. He was probably a college student and needed to study.

We continued to travel stopping in small towns to take on more passengers, and he continued to read. I saw that our journey was about to end, and I had the urge to talk to him before I ended my journey. We had one more 10-minute stop at the city of *Pirssununga,* and he put down his book. The next stop would be Araras.

I spoke to him in Portuguese, "Are you a student? I see you are reading a book on online trading. One of my grandsons just did a course on the subject."

"No, I am 'self-educated', I guess you would say, and I just paid for an expensive course on investments, too."

"Well, at your age I am sure you are trying to prepare yourself for a good financial future." I said.

"Oh, I already make a lot of money, so I want to know how to invest it. I am just so tired of traveling and being away from my little child. I would like to invest in something while I am making so much money."

I quoted some scripture about stewardship and the "love" of money.

He smiled and said, "My parents are simple folks and taught me a good work ethic. But they never emphasized education. They took me to a church, but I looked around at my peers who were going into the military or off to college and I just felt like I was stuck and going nowhere. I became a little rebellious, not at God, but with the church's attitude. So I struck out on my own."

"I make a lot of money and this book teaches to not be timid about using money. I want to teach my young daughter the right attitude about life, work and money. Most of us are very discouraged about the way our country is going."

We were getting close to Araras and my destination.

I told him, "Follow your dream and take care of your family, be thankful for your blessings, and help the new generation of Brazilians. But go back and invite Christ into your life again and into your plans and you will see that you will have more peace and security."

A thought came to me and I asked, "Are you stopping in Araras, too?" He answered yes.

"And are you here to for the *Festa do Peao*? And are you a musician*?"* I knew they make lots of money during that yearly show. Some of the top names in country music come each year before the famous rodeo.

He gave a shy smile, "Yes, *Senhora,* I go on stage tonight."

"Wow," I said. "I didn't know I was seated beside a famous person," I teased.

"I may be famous, but I am tired of this life.
Thanks for talking to me, and I promise I will think about those things we talked about. Some of the things I had forgotten."

I asked him, "I am waiting for a friend to get me. Do you need a ride?" (I really wanted to show him to Celso!)

"Thanks, but I already have a chauffeur waiting."

Later that night I could hear the loud music from the fairground that was kilometers away. I was happy that I had an opportunity to share on the bus ride. I was happy that the Lord didn't leave the bus seat empty.

******

Rose and Lilly

My most recent special moment, as I am writing this, was this week in a department store. There was no clerk in the department where other shoppers and I were, and a large, well fit man had reported the need for a clerk. We were waiting. Waiting. Finally, a nice-looking lady appeared and apologized for the delay. It was not her department, but she was there to help. We could tell that she was nervous. I was proud of the crowd as they assured her that everything would be fine now that she was there.

My purchase only came to $4.17 so they all agreed that I should go first. As the two of us were finishing the transaction, I mentioned her name tag showing her name as Sharon.

"You name is so pretty. It is a Bible name," I commented.

She touched her tag, "My name is a Bible name?"

"Yes, it is one of the names of Jesus Christ. I chose my wedding bouquet flowers to honor the names of Christ as the Rose of Sharon and the Lilly of the Valley. God already knew your name and loves you."

Tears came to her eyes, she smiled and said, "I never knew that. It will be more special to me now."

The shoppers were listening and smiled.

******

Chapter 4
Tell the Next Generation - It Works!

My son works for an insurance company whose slogan on television is: "We know a thing or two because we have seen a thing or two."

In contrast, blasphemous words echo in my head of a Brazilian man screaming at us in Portuguese in the street, "The Bible is a lie. It is false. It doesn't work. I don't want it!"

How will the next generation know that it is true? We need to share that we KNOW it is true because we have SEEN it work. We know prayer works because we have seen it work miracles. Real life, true stories help youth and adults really process the truth of God's power in prayer. Miracles can lead you to the door of faith.

It is important to pass it on to the next generation in our own families. After I told one of my granddaughters, Isabela, that my book was dedicated to my grandchildren, she said, "Grandma, we don't need to read your book because we hear about them firsthand from you."

And my children and grandchildren have their own stories to tell.

****
Lost and Found

Once, before my grandchildren had their own cars, we had moved back from Brazil and had an outing planned. We planned to leave in our family van. We were all ready to go, but where were the keys? It was time to leave, so the search began to find the keys.

The search included the van, the house, and pockets. When it was really time to go and we still didn't have the keys, I gathered the grandchildren in a huddle in the hallway.

"Kids, God knows our schedule so we need to pray that we can find the keys now."

We huddled. We prayed. Immediately after the amen, Jonathan went directly to the garage and came back smiling, holding the keys.

"Where?" we asked.

He said while we were praying the thought came to put his hands down the right side of the driver's seat and search all the way to the floor.

We were soon on our way, and one said, "Wow. Prayer works even for lost-and-found."

Yes, it works!

******

Need a Boost?

One Tuesday morning I was off to an OASIS (**O**lder **A**dults **S**till **I**n **S**ervice) meeting at 11:30 in Moore and afterward to work in Oklahoma City. Everything was organized and ready to go. But my van wouldn't start!

My cars in Brazil were standard shift. so I could put them in neutral and roll them next to another car to use a booster cable. But my automatic van was inside the garage, and I didn't know how to roll it out.

My children and grandchildren were all at work or in classes, but I sent out a text anyhow explaining my situation. I got back a response,

"Grandma, I've got this." My granddaughter Bianca had recently gotten her driver's license, and her folks had bought her a used car. She was on her way.

When she arrived, we sat in the van and I explained that the two vehicles had to be side by side to use the cables.

"I don't know how we can do that. Let's pray about it and see how God can help us." I reached for her hand and we prayed.

"Father, we love you and we are in a situation that we don't have a solution to. You know our schedule and Bianca is here to help, but I don't know what to do now. I need my van out of the garage."

Suddenly, the lights came on in the van, and the motor started running! We just looked at each other and laughed. I quickly put it in reverse to exit the garage and as soon as it was beside Bianca's car, the motor died.

She looked at me and said, "Hey, it works. But why didn't you pray to go all the way to the mechanic?"

She hopped out and was already googling the best way to use jumper cables since it was her first experience. With the boost, we made it to the mechanic. When I asked him if he could have the van ready by 1:30 pm so that I could go to work, he said, "No way, lady. It may be tomorrow." I just breathed a prayer, and Bianca took me to my OASIS meeting.

My sweet Bianca had her first experience with booster cables, but she received first-hand a spiritual boost to see that God delights in helping His children.

While I was at the meeting, the mechanic called. Guess what? He said the van would be ready by 1:30 pm.

My friend Earnie Deeds took me to the mechanic, and I was soon on my way to work.

God takes care of His children in little and big things. They knew it because they saw it.

It is true. It works.

****

A Phone Wake-Up

At one Family Reunion in the beautiful, majestic mountains of West Virginia, about 90 of the Combs family met at a 4-H Camp. My three children and four grandchildren were able to travel from Oklahoma to the reunion. On the first day, my grandson David jumped into the swimming pool with dozens of cousins trying to escape the heat. As soon as he jumped in he realized that his phone was in the pocket of his swimming trunks.

None of us had phone reception in those mountains, and it was great. We could use our phones only to photograph and record, but even with dumping his phone in dry rice kernels and using other suggested solutions, he was without his phone for the rest of the reunion.

On the way back to Oklahoma after a memorable family time, David tried his phone again after the others were getting reception on their phones. Nothing happened. He tried again.

Someone suggested, "Try praying for it like Grandma says. Maybe it will wake-up." He prayed and sure enough, the phone lit up right there in the car. The reception bars came on, and his phone was "awake" again.

They knew it because they it saw for themselves. It is true. **Prayer works!**

****

From the Mouths of Babes

Our first child was born in Brazil. I was expecting him during language school, and my vocabulary was too limited to really be able to understand all that my fast-talking Brazilian doctor told me.

Our Brazilian friends said we were *"marinheiros na primeira viagem"* (Sailors on our first voyage). We wished for family and English-speaking friends at times, but found that God's peace, a Portuguese-English dictionary, and a lot of hand gestures could help us get things right.

What we really wanted to get right was our spiritual training of our little son. We had a Christian heritage and good parenting models in our own parents concerning prayer. We found out that our baby was learning about prayer through watching us.

When Kemper was about one and a half years old, he was in his high chair at lunch waiting for the prayer before the meal. We saw him place his chubby little hands over his eyes and start praying in Portuguese. Something he had never done before.

He said, "Deus…Anita…Amen." Jim and I looked at each other in surprise. It was not our meal-time prayer, but he had heard us pray for Dona Anita who was in the hospital. We were so concerned for her because there was blood in her lungs, and they had given up hope for her recovery. We prayed for her often.

Soon they asked me to have prayer with her and her husband at the hospital. After I left the hospital, they called and informed us that she had taken a turn for the better and thanked us for our prayers. And for our baby's prayer? Soon she was released from the hospital, and for many more years she continued to be a blessing in our church.

God hears the prayers of a baby as well as our prayers. God's ways are not our ways, but He loves for us to pray boldly.

Now since my husband has gone to glory, my son lives with me. I passed by his bedroom and heard him talking. I asked him later if he were talking on the phone or talking in his sleep. He said, "You must have heard me praying."

He has come a long way from the infant prayer, but the same God hears the prayer. Pass it on to the next generation. **It works!**

****

I Told You So!

Once in Brazil we were traveling with our three small children to our home in the state of Santa Catarina from a mission meeting in the state of Sao Paulo. We had made the long road trip many times that crossed three states, but this time it was more intense.

The whole country was rationing gasoline per vehicle, and the service stations were closed on weekends. We were traveling on a Saturday.

We started out with a full tank of gas so since it was the wonderful time before iPhones and video games, we made up games for the whole family – counting horses and tractors from your side of the car, alphabet lists of things seen from the car window, listing the states from license plates, singing together, asking for "Daddy stories from when he was young and wild in the hollers of West Virginia."

The hours passed and we kept watching the gas gauge. I had packed food, but it was running low except for apple slices which I passed back to the children. Our *cacula (baby girl)* Tania had looked out the car window for kilometer after kilometer, hour after hour at the sloping hills full of banana groves.

She said in Portuguese, "There must be enough bananas in Brazil to feed everyone in heaven…and we don't have a one."

Jim and I discussed in the front seat the possibility of stopping somewhere before the gas gauge marked "empty." Cindy, our middle child, leaned forward and put her little arms on top of our front bench.

She said in Portuguese, "We need to keep going. I prayed that we would find a gas station open, and I am looking for it. Just keep going."

The faith of a child is important to Father God, so we kept going. Just before the gas gauge marked "empty," a service station appeared.

Cindy said, "See, I told you so. There it is. I told you we would find one." They also had some gasoline left and were willing to sell us some

Tell the next generation. **It works.**

******

What happens when one generation does not tell the next one?

1. Children

"But as for me and my house, we will serve the Lord."

2. Grandchildren
**"Israel served the Lord all the days of Joshua, and all
the day of the elders who outlived Joshua"**
3. Next Generations Lost
**"Another generation arose after them
who did NOT know the Lord
nor the work which he had done for Israel…
they did evil in the sight of the Lord."**
(Joshua 24:15b, 31   Judges 2:10,11)

****

E-Team in Araras, Brazil

Women Prayer Teams

"Women partnering with God"

These ladies believe
*"Prayer really
works!"*

Free Will Baptist Churches in Araras

Pastor Israel and Simone

Pastor Eliseu with Kenneth Eagleton

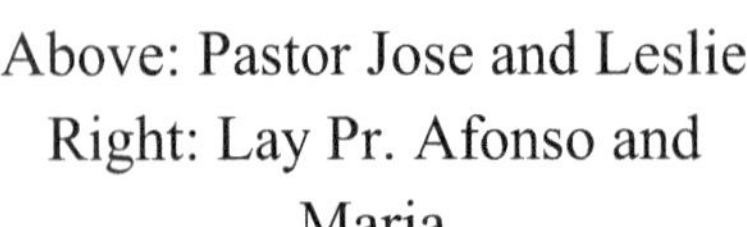

Above: Pastor Jose and Leslie
Right: Lay Pr. Afonso and Maria

Lar Nova Vida (New Life Home) *Founded in 1991 to Help Children and Their Families*

Donated Volkswagen in honor of the late missionary James Kemper Combs
"Surprise by Snail-Mail"

Family Reunions

Combs Family
West Virginia

Roberts Family
Oklahoma

The Next
Generation
Our Brazilian born
children –
Kemper, Cindy,
and Tania

The Next Generation

Our Brazilian-American grandkids – Daniel, David, Jonathan, Bianca, Julia, and Isabela

Mother-Daughter Missionary Team

Bobbie Jo Lee
Albany, Georgia

Bobbie Jean
Florida

Jiu-Jitsu
Ministry
LNV
Community
Outreach

Started by
Jim and
Bobbie Jo

PART TWO

Dusty Road Miracles

**"I have heard of you by the
hearing of the ear,
but now my eye SEES you."**
Job 42:5 (KJV)

Chapter 5
Dusty Roads

Are you ready to be amazed and maybe shocked by stories of miracles which may seem impossible or unbelievable to our modern minds? Hold on to your books because the following stories may change your thinking.

One of our daughters asked me once why we don't see healings and demon manifestations here in the US as we see them in Brazil. In some accounts in the Bible where people were possessed with demons, they are healed of physical needs as the demon leaves their bodies. (See Matthew 9:32 - mute, 12:22 – blind and mute, 17:15 - epileptic; Mark 9:17 - mute; Luke 9:38 - so torn and bruised, 11:14 - mute, 13:10 – a bent woman)

I saw the same thing in the Amazon jungle with a young naked Indian girl who was carrying a bunch of bananas on her head. My missionary friend told me that the girl was mute. We remembered her in prayer for a while. Later I received news that she was delivered of a demon when she accepted Christ, and she was now able to speak!

In my other books I have shared the story of a special child that Jim and I took from the streets of Ribeirao Preto and reared together with our other three children. They consider him their brother. In fact, they brought him from Brazil to visit with Jim before he passed on to glory, and Marco Antonio sang at the funeral of their father.

Marco helped us open the children homes later because he had lived in the streets and understood searching for food in garbage cans and being beaten by alcoholic parents. He visited our little mission church with a friend on Easter Sunday in order to get one of the chocolate Easter eggs he heard were to be given. He loved the story of the living Christ, accepted Him as Savior, and Jim baptized him. However, his father threw him out of the shanty they lived in because of his new faith, and then he was really homeless.

He is now an ordained preacher, married to a fine Christian young woman, and they have four great children. Brazil doesn't have the system of foster care, but he has been referred to as our foster son.

The following stories he has shared with me, along with before and after photos to verify each amazing fact. I have also communicated with those mentioned in his stories. God has given him a passion to deal with people one-on-one. He has about 70 homes he ministers to and lately decided that the churches in the city were not reaching out to the isolated places.

Marco Antonio and wife Claudiana decided to choose off-the-path country roads to take walks and to meet people. One afternoon they met a lady named Luzia on a dusty road. Here is her amazing story.

******

Luzia's Story

A few months ago, I was sitting in Luiza's country home as she and her husband told their amazing story to me.

On one of their walks on a dusty road near Araras, Marco and Claudiana traded greetings with Luzia who introduced herself. Marco ended up offering to pray for her for any particular need she may have. She invited them to go to her home for prayer.

One of the first things they discovered about her home was that it was full of hundreds of idols and images passed down from her great-great-grandparents. These were idols they had brought from Europe.

It was about two o'clock in the afternoon. Luzia had not told Marco that her son was sleeping in a room off the living room separated by a curtain. He drove an ambulance at night for the city government and slept during the day.

Luzia had also not said anything about being quiet, so Marco shared the Gospel in Portuguese with her in his normal, enthusiastic voice. He was sharing the truth of the Jesus of the Bible.

Suddenly Narciso her son pushed aside the curtain. He was a big, strong young man whose frame filled the doorway. He called out in Portuguese, "What is going on here that woke me up?"

Later they learned that the young man hated evangelical Christians and would release his pit bull on people he didn't want around. His mother just turned to Marco and said to continue his conversation because she really wanted prayer.

Marco told the angry man, "*Senhor,* just sit down and you will see a great surprise." He sat down.

Marco continued to tell them about Jesus and His salvation and God's marvelous works. He could feel that the family was in spiritual bondage.

"Where is the surprise? I haven't seen one surprise yet," the man interrupted.

Marco turned to the mother and asked, "We are going to pray. What is your desire?"

Marco expected her to say she wanted peace or something similar, but she said, "I want to be healed of this growth on my neck." It was the size of her open palm that now covered the growth.

Marco breathed a prayer to himself, "Okay, God. Let's go." Other family members had now joined them in the room. Marco had them all to stand with their eyes closed. He started praying, and the battle increased. A demon manifested in Luzia. Her eyes rolled back and her hair lifted in all directions.

Narciso jumped up and shouted, "Stop. Stop it. My mother is a very religious person. It is not possible that she has a demon. She prays at the feet of her images each day. Especially her patron saint, Saint Luzia. Stop it right now."

The demon addressed the son in Portuguese through the vocal cords of his mother in a low growly voice and said, "Keep quiet! You are so full of sin and fault that you can't speak now." The demon continued to tell of the man's sins that his family knew nothing about. He kept revealing sinful secrets that only Narciso knew about.

"Make him go away!" Narciso begged.

Marco told the group, "Wait there, my name is written in the Book of Life because I accepted Jesus as my Lord and Savior, but I can't use my name to tell the demon to leave."

The demon said in an ugly voice, "Too weak, your name."

Marco listed off other names he knew had no power like Saint Luzia, Saint Antonio, Saint George, the Pope, and even used the name of Elvis Presley. (Why doesn't that surprise me?)

The demon screeched out, "No, too weak, too weak!"

Marco asked if the word money was strong enough.

The demon answered, "You know the name, but I will not leave."

Marco replied, "Oh, yes, I know. It is the powerful name of Jesus Christ, and through His blood He can win. His name is above all names, and in His name all tongues shall confess."

"Now in the name of Jesus Christ and His blood, grab your misery and sadness and your ugly growth. Go away and leave this body!"

The demon let out a scream from the woman's mouth and left her body.

When Luzia was freed of the demon and out of the trance, she lifted her head and put her hand on her throat. She cried out in her own, but weak voice. "It is gone! The growth is gone."

The whole family cried out and Narciso fell on his knees.

Marco declared, 'Today salvation is coming to this house. Jesus came to bring salvation."

Their conversation continued through the night and the family members who were present accepted Christ as their Savior.

******

Marco and Claudiana were invited to return to their home so that Luzia's husband could hear the explanation of salvation. She was all dressed up and happy. Her throat was smooth and normal.

Narciso was surprised with the visit and shared with Marco a prayer request. It was about his job.

In Portugues he explained, "You know that I drive an ambulance for the city at night. I only receive about R$800 a month (about $200 dollars). I am full of debt, and we have to live with my parents. I have to work for the city for one year before I can ask for a raise."

They prayed for this need that was heavy on the heart of this new believer. Four days later Narciso called.

"I went to the bank to get the R$800 from my account. I discovered there was R$50.000 in my account. I talked to the bank people, and they said that someone deposited in my account, so they had to leave it there. It was mine."

The happy and thankful couple built them a nice house, married legally, and his wife conceived a much-wanted child.

I am thankful that I don't have to explain it, because I can't. But I can rejoice with them.

Narciso continued to drive the ambulance for the same salary. But one night he was driving a pregnant mother to the hospital. He had to stop the ambulance to help the mother deliver her baby. He had never had training but did an excellent job. People at work cheered him and suggested to authorities that they should give him special courses. Guess what? He is now the *Chefe* de *SAMU* (similar to Chief of EMT) and has a good salary.

******

Later they were invited to return for an evening meeting with the family. Another family couple said they had a prayer request. A good sign. But they wanted Marco to tell them what the request was without their revealing it. That way they could better tell if they should even be requesting it.

Marco thought, what? So he turned to everyone and told them to praise God in song and testimony. While he was praising, an image came in his mind. He was apologetic to God. He was supposed to be focusing on Him and praising and now he has allowed a vision of a tractor come to his mind. Where did that come from? Sorry, Lord.

But before the next song, Marco jokingly said, "It wasn't a tractor, was it?"

Some of the family fell to their knees. Yes! It was a tractor. They wanted to plant on their land so they could sell produce to their village.

Marco said if the thought was from God, he guessed that God was going to answer with a tractor. That week they received a tractor as a gift. Now they sell produce to their whole village.

******

Luzia's daughter came up with a prayer request. Her husband had left the family for another woman. He was the only one working, and she was left with the children with no help. She wanted prayer for him to return. They prayed. They prayed that the curse would be broken, and the husband father would return.

Later she phoned Marco, "Pastor Marco, my husband is on the front porch asking forgiveness and wants to return. What do I do?"

"Do? What did you ask God to do? Open the door and receive the answer to your prayer."

Today they are together and very happy.

******

Soon Luzia called Marco asking him to come to her house with his car. She said that she wanted him to take all of her idols and images out of her home. He filled his car and trunk with 403 idols. She said that she wanted to be totally surrendered to her Lord and Savior. As he was leaving she felt "truly of Jesus Christ."

******

There was one more son who declared to still be an unbeliever. However, Luzia asked for a service in her son's home because he was suffering with 15 kidney stones. They have socialized medicine in their country, so even though the doctors said he must have surgery, it could only be scheduled well into the future. He was in great pain.

They prayed and the pain left him. But when the surgery date arrived they still went to the doctor. After tests, the surprised doctor said that the stones were all gone.

The young man became a believer, making 18 members of Luzia's family who became followers of Jesus Christ.

There is power in the name and blood of Jesus.

******

Cristiano's Story

Another family invited Marco and Claudiana to their simple two-room home. Rain was leaking inside the house and the walls were damp. There was no stucco on the outside of their house. The wife's family didn't have much faith in the young man's abilities, and he was discouraged.

He had an old car in his a yard with no battery. He worked but he earned only R$250 a week. (About $50)

Marco started talking to the young man named Cristiano at three o'clock in the afternoon and was still answering his question at three o'clock in the morning. After twelve hours of talking about God's love and His salvation, Cristiano was receptive, and it wasn't tiresome to the two men. They started in Genesis and by the time they reached Revelation Cristiano said, "I want to accept Jesus as my Savior!" They prayed and things began to happen.

During the week they talked more about God's love, and each time Cristiano wanted to know more.

One night before dawn, Marco's phone rang. It was Cristiano. He was very agitated and said something strange had just happened.

Marco got dressed and went to their house. When he arrived, they were wrapped in a blanket waiting outside their house in the dark.

Cristiano said, "There is someone inside the house. Strange things were happening inside."

Marco went inside and there was absolutely no one in the house. He called the couple to go back inside. He asked them what was happening.

Cristiano said, 'When I went to bed, I turned off the lights. When I opened my eyes, they were turned on again. I did that two more times, and finally I got up and saw something strange. There was a shadow-like form of a terrible bad spirit moving across the room.

Marco listened then said they should pray. While they were praying there was a noise on the back porch. Marco went out in the dark and it was the washing machine making a sound like it was on the spinning cycle. But when he checked, he found that the machine was not plugged into the wall.

He felt something was very wrong in Cristiano's life.

Later Marco talked with Cristiano's mother and she said she had practiced voo-doo to "protect her son," He spent time with her, and the demon manifested and the bad spirit finally left her.

They started discipleship classes with Cristiano in his home. They shared that his wife of seven years was not able to conceive a child. The doctor had said that she had early menopause and would not be able to have children. She was in her twenties.

They started praying with Marco about their disappointment. One night during prayer she had a hard-cramping pain.

Marco said, "I would like for you to go to the pharmacy, take a simple pregnancy test, and then go to your doctor."

She went on a Saturday and the test was positive. She and her husband went to their doctor. To the glory of God, after she had more tests, she was expecting a child!

Unusual things kept happening. Another day they were sitting in the front of the house with his mother. Cristiano was grilling meat. His mother picked up a bench and moved it in front of the old car parked in the front yard. Suddenly the car motor started up all by itself, like someone was stepping on the accelerator.

Wasn't that the old car without the battery? How could it happen? I have no idea. It seemed the more the family followed the Truth in Jesus Christ, the stranger things happened around their house.

One day Cristiano opened the wardrobe in the bedroom that held clean clothes and sheets. When he was searching, he found a plate of spoiled meat with pieces of candles like they use in the cemetery. A common voo-doo sacrifice. A terrible smell.

He got a plastic shopping bag, wrapped the plate in it and closed it. (Someone was filming it.) He set fire to the bag and suddenly a wind lifted up the sack and carried it about ten meters (about 32 feet). It landed and was no longer burning. As he was striking the match about one meter away to light it again, the sack started burning again. One more strange story they had to tell.

But some things were getting better as he grew spiritually. Remember he was a bricklayer apprentice? He is now a bricklayer with lots of jobs. He has come from an old, small house to two large houses he has built in good neighborhoods. Remember the old car without a battery? He has several cars now. From a poor salary he now makes a very good salary.

Marco said, "I never preached health-wealth gospel, but I have seen God choose to prosper people as part of their transformation." Why not? He is Father God.

But Marco shared that he now had many families who needed his attention and that he was spreading himself thin. Dozens and dozens of families. He had rented a meeting place and gathered many of them together, but the rent of the building was very expensive and continued to rise. His disciples lived in so many directions in the city and surrounding areas that it was difficult for many to have transportation. So, he closed his meeting place and continues to visit home to home.

However, he felt that Cristiano needed a church with Sunday School and weekly meetings. He needed a church family to help him grow spiritually and to have opportunities to develop leadership.

Christiano found a good church for his family and has been invited to help in evangelizing and preaching. He was asked to pray for a child at church that could not walk. The child now can run around in the church.

He has come full circle and he now is going down dusty roads and reaching other families. Praise God.

*****

Chapter 6
Cobblestone Streets

Marco Antonio and Claudiana continued to meet people on their journeys down the cobblestone streets of the town, also. One of the young men they met gave them an invitation.

Renato's Story

"Can you come to my house for prayer?" Renato asked.

On Marco Antonio's first visit, he found that Renato had four main prayer requests. One was for health, another for his job, then his wife's job situation, and last to be able to conceive a child.

Let's take them one at a time.

Renato shared in Portuguese, "I have a skin problem. It is taking over my body. I can't eat a lot of things, especially pork."

He took off his shirt and showed his body covered with sores. He hid his sores with long sleeves and a cap when he went to work at the Nestle Company in town. Otherwise he feared he would be fired. No one could know about the problem, but on this visit he was asking for payer.

Marco opened the Bible and told him the story of Cornelius and Peter. Some foods prohibited in the Old Testament were shown to Peter in a vision, and he was told to eat them. When he said, "Not so, Lord!" God sent the message, "What God has cleansed you must not call common or unclean."

He explained to the troubled young man that there could be different reasons for the body to react with skin problem. But he had a question for him.

"Renato, I want you to think. Do you have any bitterness or hatred against anyone?"

He paused a moment and then looked at Marco and said, "My father. He left when I was twelve years old. Left my mother and went to Saudi Arabia. He was a professional soccer player, a goalkeeper. He did very well financially but seemed to forget all about us."

Marco read in the Bible what God says about honoring father and mother, how that bitterness was eating at him, that he needed to learn to forgive and let it go.

Somehow he got his father's phone number. The next day he called him and told him that he forgave him and loved him. They had not talked to each other in years.

The father was very emotional with the call and asked forgiveness. He said that he had accepted Christ as Savior and Lord of his life and had wanted his family's forgiveness. He had made peace with God and now he was at peace with his family. Renato sent a video to his father the next day.

He skin was changed. How could it be? Did his forgiveness and rejecting his feelings of bitterness and hate make the difference? I can't explain it, but it happened.

On a Saturday he bought a beautiful pork roast and invited Marco and Claudiana to have lunch with his family on Sunday. When they arrived and sat at the table, a nervous wife said, "Folks, he can't eat this. If he does, you will have to rush him to the hospital. He swells up and his throat closes and he can't breathe.

Tomorrow they are going to separate and fire workers at the Nestle' Company who have not studied past the eighth grade. Renato didn't finish high school. They are going to go through the list with a fine-tooth comb."

They had prayer before the meal, and all eyes were on Renato as he enjoyed his food. He ate more pork than anyone, and nothing happened. He is still free of his skin problem – it has not returned.

Now to his second prayer request: Renato had not studied past the eighth grade. The Nestle Company had implemented a new educational requirement for its workers. It is a Swiss company and treats its workers very well. Renato had already worked there many years and really depended on the job.

He went to work on Monday after the Sunday meal and prayer at his house with Marco and Claudiana He usually worked on the first floor, but when he arrived his boss asked him to work on the second floor to replace a worker who was absent. The search committee separated several workers from the first-floor workers and fired them.

Tuesday he worked downstairs on the first floor, and the search committee separated workers on the second floor and fired some.

Renato did not get fired and is still working for Nestle.

God moves in mysterious ways!

The third request was from his wife. She felt very uncomfortable working at a pharmacy where the lady boss practiced witchcraft.

She felt it was harming her marriage and thought perhaps the boss had put some kind of hex against their family.

She asked prayer for her to find a new job but was not prepared to be fired so suddenly before finding a job. Her job paid the house rent.

When she shared her situation with Marco, he told her to take her resume to the exact place that she would like to work. She took it to the *Mundial Motos* motorcycle company.

Motorcycle companies are popular in Brazil. There are probably as many motorcycles in their city as cars. The purchase price is less, and fuel consumption is less. (It has been reported that the labor cost on the production of cars in Brazil is probably the lowest in the world. However, the taxes are so high that they are some of the most expensive cars in the world. So, people invest in motorcycles as their main transportation.)

In her interview Renato's wife shared that she was a Christian now. They told her that they only hire Christians. The owner Sergio is a member of our *Igreja Batista Livre* in Araras and a fine Christian brother. She was hired. Father God is faithful.

Their fourth prayer request was something very personal. After years of marriage, the wife had not been able to conceive a child. They joined in prayer with Marco and Claudiana. They have a beautiful child now to teach one day the value of bold prayer.

Father God is faithful.

Antonio's story

Claudiana and I were invited to the store of a couple who wanted to share a wonderful story with us. The owner was busy, so his wife led us to their home in another part of the building.

When he was free, he joined us in their lovely kitchen and told us the following story. Mr. Antonio had worked at a gas station and climbed up an aluminum ladder to adjust something. It fell with him, and he hit his back. He broke a vertebra and cracked another one. He pulled out a medical document that showed he had broken his back.

The doctor said he had to have complete bed rest and that he should not make any sudden movement, or he would have to have surgery.

Marco was preaching in a church one night and saw the couple come in. The man was standing, but all bent over. When he sat he was also bent over. Time was open for prayer at the end of the service, and Antonio went forward.

He told Marco, "I can't even pick up ten pounds and I am in great pain."

Marco asked if anyone else would like prayer. A lady lifted her hand and explained that it was past time for her husband to retire. He had been trying for two years for a retirement settlement with no answers. They really had urgent needs.

He turned toward Antonio and explained that they now had two prayer requests. He was going to pray for Antonio's pain and for the lady's request. He explained that God has His own plans and His will over their lives. They will see what God's will is in both requests. Antonio agreed.

They prayed in the name of Jesus for both. The man was bent over, so Marco placed one hand on his back and one on his stomach. He prayed that the mercy of God would enter the man's life and heal him.

For the honor and glory of God, when he finished the prayer Antonio was not bent over and said he was without pain. He moved from side to side, back and forth and had no pain.

One week after he went home from that service, he was still without pain and even pushed a car to get it started.

Later he went to the doctor to have his back x-rayed to see if it were restored. He had been without pain for six to eight months, but the x-ray showed that one vertebra was still broken and another one was cracked. He played with the grandchildren and did other activities and still had no pain.

God had other kinds of miracles for Antonio's family. He eventually left the gas station and confided in Marco, "I have a dream. I would like to open a feed store with farming supplies. Would you come to my house for prayer?"

Marco went to his house for prayer and asked God's blessing on his new project, if it were His will. After the prayer Antonio said he had an old car that wasn't in very good shape that he was trying to sell to help out, but it just wasn't selling. Marco told him to put a just price on it and advertise. In three days, it was sold.

They heard that the man who wanted to retire received a letter three days later saying that the retirement had been approved!

Antonio wanted to put his feed store in the front part of his house, but it just wouldn't work. Marco suggested he put it on the market. Soon someone passed by, looked at his house, and said, "Do you want to just trade? We have a house that is too large for us and our street is very busy. You have a quiet neighborhood. Would you just trade?"

He accepted! It was a perfect size for a business and residence combined, and a place where lots of traffic passed by. He contacted companies on the Internet that sold feed for dogs, cats, cattle, etc. One contact liked him and gave a lot of counsel and support. Today he receives more than he did at the gas station.

You don't challenge God to do something through prayer. You partner with God in something that He wants to do. Feels good.

Daniel's Story

Near the city of Limeira a group of people had planned a New Year's Eve watch-night service at a camp ground. About 80 people gathered around a beautiful, crackling campfire where Marco was speaking.

A young man named Daniel drove up in a pickup. In the back he had a mattress where his paralyzed mother-in-law was lying. She had not walked in ten years after falling down a flight of stairs. Her bones had calcified, and she could only stand or lie straight. She couldn't sit.

There was praise music and testimonies, and Marco preached the New Year in until about one o'clock in the morning. They opened for prayer at the end of the service and several people requested healing for migraines, kidney problems, and other maladies. Someone carried the mother-in-law on the mattress to the middle of the circle.

Much as Jesus did, Marco asked, "What do you want with this prayer?"

She said, "I want to walk again. I want to move my arms and take care of my family. Clean my own house."

Okay, Lord. that is a big and important request from this lady. The people seated around the campfire turned on their cell phones and directed the lights toward Marco as he was praying with the lady.

"Stretch out your arm," he told her. She couldn't. When he prayed they heard popping sound like the twisting of a plastic bottle. Pop, pop. She then straightened out her arms, and then the crowd broke out in praise.

She cried, "But Marco, my legs. My legs."

He took her by the hand and helped her stand on her crooked legs. He prayed again. They heard the popping sound again and sat up with expectation, holding their phone lights toward the woman and Marco.

He prayed again and her crooked legs straightened again. She walked all around the campfire praising God along with all the other people.

Daniel was amazed but had not yet accepted Christ. He had an aunt who was also suffering. For two years she had had cancer and was bedfast. When Marco arrived at her house, Daniel was already there. He asked, "What do you folks want for Daniel's aunt?" They said they wanted Jesus to heal her or take her out of her suffering. She was a prisoner to her bed, was in a lot of pain, and couldn't care for herself.

Marco said, "Okay. God has a solution one way or another."

When he went into the room of the sick aunt there was an altar with idols. He thought to himself, "What now?"

The room was full of Catholic and Spiritist relatives, but he knew only the Truth would set the lady free. He had taken a Catholic Bible to show that the Word is the Word, and he started to preach.

He preached to her that Jesus is the Way, the Truth and the Life. Some of the family broke in and said,

"We have already called the Catholic priest, the Spiritist *Pai de Santo* and *Pai de Encosto* and nothing worked. You are talking badly about our religion and our idols."

He replied, "I am using your Catholic Bible that you consider the Word of God. God's will. Christ's will."
Then he turned to the woman on the bed and asked, "What is your belief?"

She answered, "I am a Catholic and a Spiritist."

"Have you heard of Jesus Christ?" He questioned quietly.

She answered, "Not the way you are saying."

"Do you accept Him as your Señor and Salvador?"

She replied weakly, "I accept Him now."

"Do you accept Him over these idols and reject any false god?" He asked.

"I reject, yes."

Everyone around was now respectful. She repeated quietly, "I accept Jesus as my only Savior."

Marco looked around and declared, "Today salvation has come to this house!"

Now came the hour for the miracle that Jesus had decided to do. Marco knew that Jesus was going to heal or take her. He repeated that to prepare the family.

He told the lady, "I am going to put my hand on you and pray now. Do you believe?"

She said she did. She trusted.

So, Marco prayed for the pain to go away but it didn't. She remained the same and said, "I am tired of the pain."

"So let's pray and put you in the arms of Jesus." Marco said he didn't expect what happened next. She looked up and gave a big sigh and smiled. Maybe she saw Jesus, but she went away with the angel to meet Him.

Her family marveled at the sight. For two years she suffered in pain, and they saw the immediate relief as Jesus took her.

Marco said, "Don't be sorrowful, because she is not suffering. But Jesus waited for two years, perhaps, for her to be ready to accept Him so He could take her away with Him to heaven."

That day the entire family knelt and accepted Jesus as their Savior, including her nephew, Daniel. Praise God.

Now God had a big answer for Daniel. He was growing in his new faith, but he soon met difficulties. Later he called and said he was without work. Necessities were growing, they were almost without food, and they had started to quarrel. His wife was even talking about a separation.

Marco asked, "Have you put in your resume?"

"Oh, yes, in many places." So, they prayed and put the request before God.

He went back to the very best workplace where he had gone before with his resume to apply for work. The day he went to the company, a lady was leaving the building.

He asked, "*Senhora,* where do I take this resume'?"

"Let me see it," she said. She read it and said she liked the profile. He later discovered she was an important person in that firm.

She said, "Come here tomorrow, and we will talk. "

The next day he went and was hired immediately. Today he receives a very good salary, He and his wife are happy together, and they are praising God for His marvelous works.

****

Fernando's Story

Claudiana and I clapped at the gate of the family who had requested a visit. They met us with smiles and led us through a garage with a nice car and motorcycle and then into a lovely furnished living room.

The story they were about to share with me told me of a very poor and devastating beginning for this family. We sat together on the sofas and Fernando and Elaine shared their testimony of how their lives were drastically changed.

Fernando told how he used to be an alcoholic which left his family with little food and without an appropriate home.   One day he was trying to sell his CD player to take money to his family. Marco Antonio heard him talking about it and asked to be able to go to his house to look at it. He said when Marco got to his simple little house Marco admitted that he was more interested in praying for him then in seeing his CD player.

Fernando told me, "That really made me nervous I told him that I didn't want his prayers. People had already come to my house with prayers – priests and evangelists – and promised transformation and change and nothing happened. I told him to just look in my refrigerator and see if anything changed. "

Marco looked into his refrigerator and saw only water and a bottle of mustard.

Marco Antonio told him, "If you will just go to the church service Saturday evening, listen to the Gospel, repent and surrender your life to Jesus Christ, you will see change. I guarantee it."

Fernando insisted, "I don't believe you and I don't want your prayers."

"Look, you just go there Saturday and surrender to Christ and you will see…," Marcos said.

Fernando interrupted, "I won't be there…unless it rains."

Marco insisted, "I guarantee that by Monday you will see great changes in your life, if you surrender to Christ on Saturday. If not, I will eat this Bible with that water and mustard that are in your refrigerator."

Fernando said, "You show up here Monday and if nothing has happened, I'll smash in your face!"

Well, it rained Saturday and Fernando reluctantly went to the service. He listened to the preaching, he understood, and prayed to surrender to Christ.

The next day he felt impressed to look for a better house to rent for his struggling family. As he walked around one neighborhood, he saw a lady leaving a nice house. He approached her and asked, "*Senhora,* would you happen to know of a house to rent?"

She replied, "Well, I live in *Sao Paulo* and come here each month to check on my house. I don't know much about my neighborhood now. I am considering whether to rent this house or not."

"Oh, I am an evangelical Christian now and I promise to take care of it if you would consider me," he said. (He was a Christian for one day.)

"Really, you are?' I am too. Well, I could give you a good price. How about BR$500?" she offered.

"I know that is a good offer, but I couldn't pay that," he said.

"How much can you pay, then?" she asked.

He thought a moment, "Oh, about BR$180."

She looked up surprised, but after a moment agreed.

And by Sunday morning Fernando had a better house for his family!

Now he needed to find a job. That same morning, he went to the Copacabana Supermarket and looked for the manager.

"I'm looking for a job and wonder if you have any need for a worker. I am an evangelical and will do a good job for you. "

"You are? I am, too. If you know how to drive, I need a driver to deliver on Saturday and Sunday. We close early on Sunday for church. I pay BR$400 on Saturdays and BR$400 on Sundays."

"Okay, I'll take it. But I have a request. I need food in my refrigerator and in my cabinets for my family so could you advance me credit before I work so I can buy food for you to deduct from my first payment."

They granted that favor and Fernando took BR$600 worth of groceries to his family that night.

So by Monday God had made great changes in his life. He was moving to a better house, he had a job, and his refrigerator held more than mustard and water. And his family was rejoicing with their new husband and father.

Marco Antonio was rejoicing once again that God showed up with transformation and he didn't have to eat his Bible with water and mustard.

As we were leaving, Fernando and his wife's last words to me that day were, "Thank you for being the spiritual mother of Pastor Marco Antonio. He brought the power of a transforming God into our lives." Amen, Fernando!

Pastor Marco
Antonio Pena
Wife,
Claudiana
Children,
Jesse',
Victoria,
Suzana, and
Ana Carolina

Luzia - Aparecido

Antonio with wife and daughter

Aparecido &Elaine

**Pastor Marco
And His
Disciples**

Renato

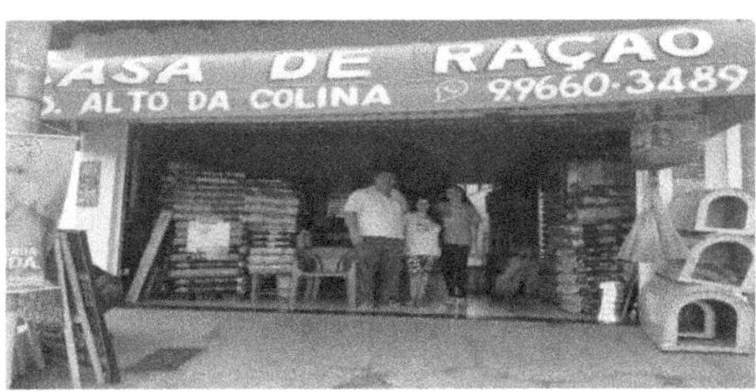

PART THREE

This and That

"Now unto him that is able to do exceeding abundantly above all that we ask or think, according to the power that works in us."
Ephesians 3: 20

Chapter 7
Where's the List?

I am a list maker. A to-do list. A grocery list. A prayer list.

I am flexible, too. If it doesn't get done today, I circle it for tomorrow. If the market doesn't have an item, I circle it for the next trip. If a prayer is answered, I put the date and praise marks. If one isn't answered, it stays on the list, and I just wait patiently while God is putting things into motion.

Empty Suitcases

After 44 years as residents of Brazil, I found myself struggling with a difficult list. We were allowed two suitcases each for our re-entry into the United States, but how do you pack 44 years into four suitcases?

Jim thought it would be easier to include the furniture when we put our house for sale. Also included in that sale were pots and pans, dishes, sheets and towels, and even the décor on the walls. Jim gave away his tools to friends, and I gave to our Brazilian leaders my teaching and research materials, child evangelism illustrated lessons, and books that were written in both Portuguese and English.

Clothes and shoes? There was no Brazilian culture for yard sales, but we placed our shoes and accessories on tables and hung our clothes on makeshift clothes lines and invited our church family and friends to help themselves. Some suggested that we put at least a small price so that one person wouldn't take everything.

We put the equivalent of fifty cents on each item. All that was left was what we had packed to take with us.

We were able to just turn our backs on things to leave behind, but the hardest part was saying goodbye to people and the ministry we were leaving behind.

A missionary arrives in an area to work himself out of a job, a little different than a pastor's agenda. He trains the national people to eventually take over. Then he moves on to a new work in that town or possibly in another city suggested by the Field Council of missionaries.

In our last city of ministry, we left three Free Will Baptist Brazilian churches in the competent hands of Brazilian leadership. The two houses of the Lar Nova Vida Children's Home had a Brazilian Board of Directors and Christian workers.

We served as we were invited by our national leaders. We had retired from the Free Will Baptists International Missions (IM) four years before and had chosen to continue to live and serve in Brazil. To train. Train, Train.

We had considered what that meant. We lost our two salaries and all the blessings of benefits provided by our accounts with IM. But our house and car were paid for, and we received our Social Security checks in dollars which we exchanged for the local currency. When we retired, the exchange rate was about $1.00 USD to R$4.00 BR. Four years later it had dropped to $1.00 USD to R$2.00 BR. A real budget squeezer.

My husband was often invited to preach at the three churches and was a mentor and counselor to the leaders. I was invited to conduct seminars for women's groups and to help the leaders prepare material for special events, camps, and Vacation Bible School. I assisted in mentoring the workers and administrative staff at Lar Nova Vida Children's Home.

We were careful to keep a low profile and help behind the scenes, but we were busier than ever. And we felt loved, useful, and respected by our community and by our national leadership.

However, my husband and partner in ministry seemed restless. Was it the currency exchange? Were the ministries in good hands? Was it because our Brazilian-born children were 5,000 miles away with their growing families?

He couldn't tell me.

My home church is Rejoice Free Will Baptist Church in Owasso, Oklahoma. They flew us back to attend their 50th Anniversary celebration. I was a charter member there in my teens since my parents, Rev. W. T. and Marie Roberts, started the church in that community.

The pastor Leonard Pirtle reminded me that there is a season for everything. If God gives us a green light to return to the US, then doors will open for ministry with our family and among Christian ministries in the United States.

I kept these things in my heart first and prayed about the possibility of a big change. A big fact for me in favor of returning to the US was that during different seasons of our lives our children and their families were either living in Brazil while Jim and I were on stateside assignment from IM, or they were in the United States in Bible Colleges while we were in Brazil.

Now they were all living in Moore, Oklahoma, where they had lived as children while we were directors of the Missions Department at Randall University.

I finally shared with my husband that I was praying about a big change. Transformation! I just sat back and watched. He loved Brazil and the people as much as I do. It was his idea to stay in Brazil after retiring. He had fishing buddies, chess buddies, and many friendships beyond our church families. He spoke the language well and also spoke the heart language of the people. But a change came over him.

While my heart was heavy and hurting with the thought of all we were leaving, his heart was light just planning on what we could be facing.

Re-Entry – Empty List

After I prayed through, a burden was lifted. This adventure was too big for me, so I didn't even make a list. I just felt numb, or was this peace? I just surrendered to each day's leading. After all, the Word says that God is able to do exceedingly abundantly above all that I could ask or think, so why not just let Him make the lists from now on.

The yellow caution light had just turned green, but what to do next? When we moved to Brazil for the first time in 1964, we had raised money to cover renting a house, buying minimal furniture, the cost of language school, a ministry budget, and eventually a car. But for re-entry into the US, we had very little. But as they say, "Little is much if God is in it."

Before we left for Oklahoma, our niece, Lancia, offered us a Van for $1,500. Jim paid for it right away, and it was waiting on us when we arrived the day after

Thanksgiving in 2008. God's list had already started, and He had more surprises for us.

For a while we lived with our children in Moore. Soon our brother-in-law Jim Puckett took my husband to his bank to ask for a loan to buy a house. Rejected. We owed no one and had no credit since we had lived outside the US for 44 years.

Rejected.

We checked out HUD (repossessed) homes first. We had only a small amount for a down payment, but we made a bid on one of their homes. They weren't very encouraging since our bid was low, but we just waited to see what God had on His list.

A few days later we were at my sister Carolyn's home in Skiatook, Oklahoma, when we received a call from the bank. "Mr. Combs, we are calling to advise you that your bank loan was approved, after all."

Yes! Thank you, Jesus.

Two hours later HUD housing called, "Mr. Combs, did you like the house on NE 18th Street in Moore?"

He answered, "Yes, it needs a lot of work, but it was our first choice."

"Well, even though your bid was lower than the others, you have been approved."

Yes! Thank you, Jesus.

Finally, after spending thousands to repair the house, we had a US address, a home. But empty.

Empty House – Another List

Friends and family and yard sales were great to help us find the essentials to put in our newly prepared home.

Soon the home was filled with beds, dressers, sofas, tables and chairs, and even clothes in the closet. The missionary provision closet from IM in Nashville, Tennessee, opened its doors for retiring missionaries, and soon we had our van loaded with pots and pans, sheets and towels, and even wall décor. Sound familiar? All that we had left behind in Brazil, was given back to us.

Culture Shock – Empty Agenda

Travelers and new missionaries are informed about culture shock. The language barrier in a foreign country reduces you to baby talk. Food and climate are different. Strange holidays. Are they pagan or not? You may feel the lack of your US holidays and all that is involved with celebrations.

Everywhere you turn there are adjustments.

But God still had more lists. We left behind a lifetime of friends and family. As soon as we arrived in Oklahoma on the day after Thanksgiving to share a holiday meal with our children and grandchildren, our lives began to fill with our family and friends. Once again we could talk, sing, worship, and laugh in our own native tongue – English.

Well, except for strange expressions: bff, brb, ty, ttyl, yw, thx and lol. (I thought that lol meant lots of love.) Lol!! The difference between Tweet and Twitter? Siris and Google?

I now enjoy having hot water in all the sinks, a clothes dryer, and heat and air everywhere, even in the stores and churches. But I had to learn how to use a self-serve gas pump, how to text on a bigger phone.

Had to learn the difference between Messages, Messenger, and WhatsApp. I learned how to edit and send photos right from my phone. I felt that was amazing.

You hesitate to admit that you have never deposited a check at a drive-through, and that you had to learn to punch all the no-no-no buttons just to get a simple car wash.

Since our cars in Brazil were always standard shift, it was nice to go to an automatic and learn to use cruise control. Nice.

If you had never shopped with a debit or credit card, questions like slide? Chip? Cash return? Punch yellow or green? One furlough was the first time I heard the question "Paper or plastic?" Uh, I'm sorry, but can you repeat that, please?

Church Bench

Some retirees feel the adjustment of identity. In the box to give your profession do you write "retired teacher," "retired nurse," or "retired missionary"? Or do you just mark "retired"? Some feel cut off from part of their history. Others feel freedom to look to new history. Others are still in the process of defining who they really are for the rest of their life chapters.

One small thing we soon noticed was that we were cut off from the private correspondence from our missionary headquarters that goes to the active missionary families. Okay, so we went online to feel that pulse and heartbeat of what God was doing across the planet. We just needed to feel connected, to belong.

We chose Kingsview FWB church where some of our children were attending.

We fell in love with the people and their vision as a church. At first we enjoyed just sitting on the church bench and worshiping together in our own native language. Waiting to see how God wanted us to serve.

We had come from 44 years of training our native leaders, translating and providing materials for them to use in ministry. Mentoring and counseling. Serving behind the scenes when it would have been easier and faster to just do it ourselves. We were transporting people to their homes when there were no more buses after a late meeting. So we enjoyed the church bench – for a while.

Full Agenda - Ministry

A new friend in our Sunday School class, Pat Fish, invited us to sing in the Community Joy Choir of about 25 people from several churches. The choir visits once a week to sing in hospitals, assisted living centers, and memory care homes. There were about six members from our Sunday School class who were part of the Joy Choir. It was a good fit for us since we enjoyed singing and loving on the elderly, handicapped, and their caregivers.

Our Sunday School class teacher Earnie is the president of a monthly meeting of older leaders called OASIS (Older Adults Still In Service). We soon started participating and renewed fellowship with retired lay people, preachers, deacons and their wives. At that time, it met at our church, and Jim and I became part of the host team that prepared the meals and set up and took down the tables and chairs. Soon I was offered the opportunity to be their activity director. Another good fit for us.

Later we were given opportunities to help in the church nursery on Wednesday evenings. Then came invitations to teach in Vacation Bible School and to teach three- to five-year-olds in Sunday School. We formed a Women Active for Christ (WAC) day meeting for mission-minded prayer warriors.

Jim received opportunities to preach in various churches, and for a year and a half he preached two and three times a week in one church.

A couple in Albany, Georgia, blessed us with tickets to return to our beloved Brazil to spend a month each year. A highlight for us.

Full Agenda – Family

We arrived in Oklahoma in time to be with our children and grandchildren from kindergarten to high school. Sports events, music concerts, class plays, Grandparents' Day, and we attended their high school graduations.

We couldn't be present for our children's college graduations since we were continents apart, but we proudly saw two Brazilian-born grandchildren graduate with honors from Randall University in Oklahoma, another studied there, and one is studying there now at the time of this writing.

Since Jim is from a large family scattered throughout the US, we enjoyed the Combs Reunions, usually meeting in beautiful West Virginia. We had a lot of catching up to do.

*****

Reverend Henry Braisher and Reverend EarnieDeeds

Chapter 8
What's Behind the Bend?

Two days after Thanksgiving 2016 at our daughter Cindy's house, Jim went to his VA doctor on a Saturday morning with a tummy ache. I offered to go with him, but he told me to go on to work at Wood Creations showroom, and he would call later. My work would be close to the VA Hospital in Oklahoma City. So, I went to work not knowing what a heartbreaking day that would be.

By the afternoon with no word from him, I called his number. He answered with, "Well, honey, I have been taking tests for hours."

I asked, "What are they finding?"

Then came the answer we were not prepared for. "They say I have stage four cancer, and I have three to four months to live."

My son-in-law, Rodrigo, passed by my counter at that moment and asked, "What's wrong?"

After I told him he said, "Go right now to the hospital, and I will close up and be there soon."

I guess he called our other children because soon we all surrounded the bed of the man who had always been healthy and happy. We had recently traveled to Brazil, and he left a little earlier than I did to return to his job helping handicapped students on and off their special school bus. So full of life and plans. We had one more financial obligation to pay, and he wanted us to quit our jobs and travel to visit family and friends. Our bucket list had a hole in it.

God had another travel plan for Jimmy Kemper Combs just two months later. We had shared 23 addresses together for almost 54 years when God changed Jim's to a new address. A move I couldn't make with him. He left his body for me to bury so that he could go on to glory in the afternoon of February 7, 2017. The family was in the living room, and I was on the bed with him holding his hand and I watched him take his last breath before I called them to his bedside.

We celebrated his life on February 11, at Randall University in Oklahoma, with about 500 family and friends present, but still in a little shock at the suddenness of it all.

The Last Laugh

But Jim taught us how to look at death with his songs, silly jokes, and funeral plans. At the hospital he told the room full of doctors and nurses who had given him the news that he only had three to four months to live, "I need another doctor."

They looked at each other and told him he could certainly ask for another opinion. He said, "I need a Dr. Pepper." The young medical group laughed and guaranteed him that he could have all the Dr. Pepper he wanted. Our grandson Jonathan was there and quickly left and returned with a two-liter bottle.

Brazil didn't have Dr. Pepper or Mexican restaurants, so as soon as we arrived in the US for stateside assignment, he wanted Taco-Bell and Dr. Pepper. Some friends even dropped Dr. Pepper bottle caps into his casket.

During the last days of his life, while sitting in a chair on the stage at Randall University chapel, he shared his testimony with students and faculty about living and dying. On Sunday morning he preached sitting in a chair at Iron Chapel FWB church, and on Sunday evening he preached at Dibble FWB Church. He participated there in his last Lord's Supper and feet washing service. He soon spent more days in his recliner and in bed planning his funeral.

His spiritual children and co-workers from Brazil called him often, and two friends from our Araras churches, Pastor Jose Assuncao and Sergio Leal, visited him a few days before he passed. Brazilians were shocked and grieving because we were continents apart. He ended up comforting them over the phone with the hope of eternal life with God after death.

He never lost his humor and liked to keep others entertained with his funny stories and songs. But we shared moments alone where he had tears in his eyes as he sang about heaven. One night I woke up and noticed he was still awake.

"What is it, honey? Are you hurting?" I rolled toward him and touched his shoulder.

"No. I can't talk about it right now. It is good and it is sad."

I just waited in case he wanted to talk about it.

"I heard a voice calling my name," he whispered.

Was it an angel calling him? Had his time come?

He continued, "I heard it clearly. It was my mother's voice. She said, '*Jimmy Kemper, you get up here right now or I will beat you half to death*'." Well, it wasn't an angel after all.

Maybe he realized I wanted to giggle because he said it really was his mother's voice, and it was so wonderful. We talked a while about relatives and friends who are waiting for us in heaven. Our hope was greater than it had ever been because heaven was more real than it had ever been. What a Hope we have as children of God!

As he planned his funeral, he kept his humor. While choosing his music he called his Aunt Kate in South Carolina. She was already in her mid-nineties, and they were very close. They could always find something to laugh about. He had stayed with her and her military husband at one time while he worked in Washington, D.C., and learned to appreciate classical music from her. She was a refined Christian lady, a prayer warrior, and an accomplished pianist.

On the phone he said, "Aunt Kate, I guess you heard my news."

"Yes, Jimmy Kemper, I did, and I have been praying for you."

"Well, I had always thought you would go to heaven before I did, but it looks like my call has come first," he said.

"I never thought you would go first, either. But you can tell Cecil and Norma (his parents) hello for me, and tell them I'll be there soon," she said seriously.

"Aunt Kate, I called to tell you that Tennessee Ernie Ford is going to sing at my funeral," he said changing the mood of the conversation.

"Oh, dear. Are you hallucinating, Jimmy Kemper? He is already dead, isn't he?" She asked.

Teasingly he answered, "Oh, he will be singing *'Come on Down, Lord Jesus* – on CD."

That was the last time they talked together, and Aunt Kate wasn't there to hear Tennessee Ernie sing, but she has now joined Jim in heaven and maybe they are laughing together with joy.

We had just had a good visit with Jim's family in West Virginia a few months earlier. Knowing his time was so short, he chose not to travel, but let those who could, come visit him here. He had visitors from many places.

Just before Christmas 2016, Jim's sister and brother-in-law Nancy and Ed Cook came to visit him from Kentucky. While in Oklahoma, they stayed in the home of Jim's other sister and brother-in-law Judy and Jim Puckett who live in Norman, just 10 miles south of us. Both Jim Puckett and Ed are pastors, so our lives and theirs have intertwined through the years, and we are very close.

During their visit, Judy and Jim invited us and others to their home for a Christmas celebration. Tania's in-laws Mardem and Maria Ferreira and two grandsons were visiting them from Brazil. The Pucketts' children and grandchildren who live locally, our family members, and all of those from Brazil and Kentucky gathered for an evening of snacks, visiting, and games.

Near the end of the evening, we gathered in the living room and Jim sang acapella ***"Come on Down, Lord Jesus."*** Several were recording both audio and video on their phones, and there wasn't a dry eye in the house. It seemed to be his way of saying goodbye to everyone.

Jim asked Pastor Ryan Giles and Pastor Lewis Cox to participate in our celebration of his life.

He asked me to put a tiny message in an empty walnut shell and place it in his casket. He arranged with Pastor Lewis to take out the walnut and read the message at the funeral.

It read: "The shell is empty, but the nut is already gone!"

Everyone laughed at Jim's last joke, and he would have been pleased.

Other speakers were part of our story: Clint Morgan from IM (International Missions) ; Curt Holland from IM who was "adopted" by our family while he and his family worked in Brazil; Rabbi Osvaldo Garagorry from Colorado who was our seminary student in Brazil; and two of our children, Kemper and Cindy.

Our children arranged for our foster son Marco Antonio to arrive from Brazil in time to visit Jim during his last days. Marco sang at the funeral, *"Milagre Sou"* (I am a Miracle), and gave his miracle testimony from being a street child, then coming to live with us, to finally becoming an ordained minister who continues to work in our beloved Brazil. His English is limited, but he represented what missions is all about.

A musical highlight that he didn't plan was the moment a Brazilian choir of our spiritual children from the three churches in Araras was projected bigger than life on the screen. They were led by Pastor Jose Assuncao. They told me later that they met the night before and practiced until about 11:00 p.m. to be able to send it secretly to our children in time for the funeral. It was a surprise for me, and I came unglued at their outpouring of love.

Some commented they had never seen a funeral like his. Jim planned most of it, but if he had been there he would have complained that it was too long!

"Blessed are they that weep, for they shall be comforted." Words of Jesus and so true.

Empty Chair – New Normal

Like many other ministry widows, I started on a chapter of my "new normal." Fortunately, I was still healthy enough to continue many of my activities, but now I would continue without him.

About four months after his home going, I was given a round-trip ticket to Brazil for three months. I found our friends there were still grieving and needed to hear his positive attitude about his home going. It was a fruitful three months.

The poem The ***Bend in the Road*** by Helen Steiner Rice was sent to me, and I found it has good advice.

Sometimes we come to life's crossroads
And we view what we think is the end,
But God has a much wider vision
And He knows that it's only a bend

The road will go on and get smoother
And after we've stopped for a rest,
The path that lies hidden beyond us
Is often the path that is best.

So rest and relax and grow stronger,
Let go and let God share your load
And have faith in a brighter tomorrow -
You've just come to a bend in the road."

After I returned from Brazil, it seems the invitations I received to speak at events were a little different. Had God made a change in His lists?

Only a few days after I arrived, I spoke at a District WAC meeting in McAlester, Oklahoma. The difference there was that some pastors were present, and they invited me to speak at Sunday morning services in their churches. Invitations took me to several churches in the state. One pastor invited me to speak weekly on prayer which lasted eight weeks. I had traveled to Colorado to speak at the 14th anniversary of the Aliyah Congregation of Messiah Jewish believers, and later to the Texas State Meeting of Free Will Baptists. There was a lot to see after the bend in the road.

Empty Budget

If it were not for the miracles that God did in my budget, I would not want to talk about this subject.

In September when I returned from my months in Brazil, Wood Creations had downsized. So instead of working, I returned to my activities with Joy Community Choir and OASIS (Older Adults Still in Service).

I had never really thought about how death affects your financial budget – the income drops to one half! Your insurances and taxes remain the same, and so do house payments and utility bills. I downsized on some nonessential items, but on paper it would not balance out. How do you adjust?

Prayer. When God gave us the green light to return to the US, I told Him I would rest in Him. And I really did. I didn't mention finances to anyone, and I just took each day in peace. But my children volunteered to help for a while as much as they could.

In October I received a phone call from a Ms. Olga from Dallas, Texas. It was a job offer from an E.C.I. school that teaches English as a second language. Where? On the campus of Randall University (RU) right in the city where I live. RU has provided classrooms for this school, and now they were offering me a part-time job for six months.

My students were from Russia, France, and Colombia. God brought a little mission field to me. My son Kemper helped prepare the students for the TOEFL Test (an English-speaking proficiency test), so the two of us had to say bittersweet goodbyes as the students went back to their various countries at the end of their course.

While I was without a job God sent help in little ways. One day I scratched down my grocery list to fit my budget and then started out the door for my supermarket which is only two streets away. The doorbell rang. It was a Christian friend with a gift card to the very supermarket where I was going to shop. Wow, did I splurge, and I had a balance left over for another trip. Thank God for Christians who listen to God's voice. I am glad my heavenly Father is rich and generous.

Five months after my last job, I received another phone call. It was Dr. Mark Brashier from Randall University. They were offering me a job as receptionist. I went by his office for an interview, sort of, and told him about my appointments already scheduled. He said, "No problem." I told him about my yearly trip to Brazil. "No problem," he said. So, once again God had a surprise on His list for me.

The student leaders at RU asked me to help them host the many international students enrolled that year. Students from England, Wales, Australia, Africa, China, Mexico, and Brazil. My daughters Cindy and Tania helped me cook for them and collect blankets, furniture, and other needed items for them.

The Cultural Night dinner was a success and brought everyone close together as we shared international food dishes, songs in different languages, cultural habits, and games. There were seven soccer players from my beloved Brazil, and that was a bonus for me. They even honored my request that they sing their national anthem in Portuguese for the whole group.

At the same time another blessing we received was the arrival of a young dentist Fabio Jodas, his wife and tiny twin boys from our hometown in Araras, Sao Paulo. He was studying at the University of Oklahoma. They had been friends of our Lar Nova Vida Children's Homes there. It was good to be able to help them get adjusted and to see our country from their eyes.

It reminded us that "God so loved the world that He gave His only begotten Son…" and for that reason we were all gathered together in Jesus' name at a Christian University.

Once again my re-entry led me to a mission field right at my doorstep. He still supplies all my financial, emotional, and physical needs. He has answered so many prayers and allowed me to see dreams come true. He has taught me that waiting as He works is worth it all.

After the bend of the road, God has great things on His list. At my age I have gladly made the following my prayer.

"Now also when I am old and gray headed,
O God, forsake me not:
UNTIL
I have shown **thy strength** unto this generation,
And **thy power** to everyone that is to come."
Psalm 71:18 (KJV)

Chapter 9
A Young Mother's Story

(Translated from Portuguese)

Claudiana Vasconcelos Pena, Christian wife of our foster son, shared the following story with me. She wrote:

Seven years ago, I discovered I was expecting another child. It really took me by surprise as well as my whole family because I already had another small child. I was already the mother of three children. Victoria was 15 years old; Jesse was ten, and Suzana was five. I had to take four exams for me to believe it. I was expecting another baby!

But finally, we knew there really was a precious being growing inside of me. At first my youngest daughter was jealous, but as the months passed, everyone got accustomed to the news.

Everything was going well with the baby and with me. I didn't know the gender yet, but at the seventh month we discovered it was a little healthy girl.

When it came time for another ultrasound, the doctor confused the date and marked a cesarean for March 3, 2013.

My husband, my oldest daughter, my mother and I went to the hospital happy about the soon arrival of our new baby, I went to the hospital confident and believing in Jesus that everything was going to be fine.

I said goodbye to my husband and daughter who had to go quickly to a neighboring city and would return soon to see our newborn daughter. My mother stayed with me.

Soon I was in the delivery room for surgery. Then something happened. My baby was born and then died!

Her heart stopped. Everyone went into action to revive her since every second would be crucial to saving her. But they were having trouble. Finally, my baby daughter's weak pulse returned, and they took her straight to the Natal ICU Unit.

I stayed in the surgery room without knowing what was happening. When my husband and daughter returned to see the baby, the news hit him like a bomb. His world took a leap at the moment he heard the diagnosis from the doctor.

The doctor said, "Dad, unhappily your daughter's heart stopped. Her lungs were not formed properly, and she didn't get oxygen to her brain."

My baby daughter didn't move even one muscle, nor did she cry. She breathed only through oxygen tubes.

The doctor continued, "If she happens to survive she will

- Not speak,
- Not walk,
- Not be able to see,

And summing it up, she will just vegetate. All that medicine can do for her, we have done, and now only a miracle from God can save her. Because the doctor delivered the baby before it was time…"

While the doctor was talking, my husband quit listening to him and walked to the incubator and put his hands inside and covered the tiny feet of our baby girl, and prayed to Jesus.

At that moment our baby started to move. The doctor said it must have been a type of spasm, a convulsion. He didn't realize that Jesus was placing everything in its place.

To make the situation even worse, after four days I was taken back to the hospital again. I had gone home, and my baby had stayed in the Natal ICU. I was suffering post-partum complications – between life and death.

Summing it up, both my baby and I would have died. It was a time of suffering for my whole family. But God is the God of impossibilities and He always will be.

For a person who was supposed to vegetate or die, today she glorifies the name of Jesus Christ. She is now six years old. Today she

-speaks,

-reads like an adult,

-plays and runs,

-is intelligent and gets "A's" at school and mainly, she loves Jesus.

She and I were healed. Jesus Christ is really marvelous. God transforms the crying into happiness, loss into victory.

Her name is Ana Carolina, which means "full of God's grace." My family is a testimony of this miracle and many others of how wonderful God is. May my testimony serve for many people that today are suffering and have already lost hope.

God is the same yesterday, today and forever. The God of miracles.

"I am the resurrection and the life; he who believes on Me, even though he dies, yet he will live again…" John 11; 25, 26

Claudiana Vasconcelos Pena
Araras, Sao Paulo, Brazil

*****

Little Lucas's Story

During my third session to speak at our Tuesday afternoon prayer meeting in Araras, the women reported a miracle answer to their prayers.

Little Lucas was born with an eye allergy infection that was causing him great pain at eight years old. The doctor said if he continued to rub his eyes from the constant itching, he could go blind!

After he heard his grandmother's many prayers he declared to her, "*Vovo', o milagre ja' vem.*" Grandma, the miracle is coming soon." And the miracle did come.

When he returned for a check up to confirm the miracle, the doctor declared, "The disease is gone. There is not even any scar tissue left."

The little boy's faith continues to grow. Recently he was in the city's botanical park with his family. When the grandmother told him it was time to leave, he said, "But Grandma, we can't go. I haven't talked to anyone about Jesus yet."

"Well, we can wait one more hour before we leave for you to talk to someone," she conceded.

"Thanks. Jesus sent people in groups so I am going to take my little cousins with me."

They left hand in hand and went to other families gathered in the park and spoke to them one-by-one. What tiny little witnesses in the park that day.

His teacher shared with Lucas' family about an incident the other day in school. He saw a little classmate sad and alone and asked her, "Teacher, may I take my sad friend outside for prayer?"

She said yes and he did just that. It was like the healing of his eyes gave him spiritual eyes of compassion at eight years old to see the special needs of others

"Out of the mouth of babes comes perfect praise." Matthew 21;16, Psalms 8:2

*****

Chapter 10
Word Whispers

During the years of my walk-through life I have had words/urges pop into my mind and I have learned to recognize the voice of my Good Shepherd. I have shared those with others and now here are some recent ones.

"Step Outside"

Years ago, I wanted to make it a habit to share hope with someone each day. That would depend on meeting up with someone and some days I didn't meet anyone. However, usually there was a meaningful cell phone call that would give me an opportunity.

A few months back I sang the words, "Lord, lay some soul upon my heart and love that soul though me," as I was cleaning house. I suddenly had an urge/thought: *"Step outside the door"*. Okay. It was about 90 degrees and it was too early to go to the mailbox, but I stepped out into the hot Oklahoma sunshine.

I walked around a little, checked on my rock garden (which doesn't need water and does well in sunshine), and looked around the neighborhood. A young man wearing a ball cap was passing in front of my house pushing an old, old clacking lawn mower. He wasn't looking at me so maybe it wasn't he who the Lord was sending. He kept passing, looked my way, and saw me looking at him. He called out asking if I needed my lawn mowed. I motioned him to come closer.

I asked if he lived close by, and he said he did. I explained that my son, grandsons, and son-in-law mow my lawn for me since my husband passed on to glory. When I asked the price, he gave a number that was half what most charged. Okay, he must be the one, so I agreed for him to mow.

After he started mowing, I went into the house to get him some cold water. By the time I returned to take him the water, I didn't hear the clack-clack of his old machine. He was sitting on the curb with some tools in his hands.

"Are you out of gas?" I asked.

"No, this piece fell off and I was trying to put it back on, but it may need to be replaced," he offered.

I watched him work on the piece for a while then offered to allow him to finish the yard with my lawn mower. I told him it was full of gas.

He said he had the gas but would like to finish the job for me. I took him to the backyard shed where he took out the mower. Soon I heard my mower purring around, and soon he was finished and at my front door. I invited him in for more cold water.

I asked him name and he told me it was Michael.

"That's a good Bible name, an angel," I said.

"Yes, Michael the Archangel. I have heard two different stories, and I don't know which to believe," he said.

He told me a strange story about the ministry of Michael in helping Jesus in ministry. I listened and felt that here was the reason that God brought the young man to my street. I asked him if he wanted me to tell him the Bible teaching about Jesus, the salvation story, and about Michael. He said he would like to hear it.

He listened politely and asked a few questions. He said that he and his father were alone taking care of his mother who was suffering from dementia and talked about the challenges they were having. I asked him for prayer requests, and we prayed together.

When I paid him, a little more than he asked, I wondered if we would ever meet again. After he left, I looked around at my lawn and realized he had carried off brush and trash that I had trimmed from my trees and bushes and had done more than just mow my lawn. I was glad I paid him extra.

I may not see him again, but I know God loved him enough to send him my way that day. And I am glad I "stepped out the door."

"Stop Here"

It was after nine o'clock at night and I was returning from taking fruit to Lar Nova Vida Children's Home in Araras, Sao Paulo, Brazil. The rain had stopped, and the temperature was back up to the 90's so I was ready for a bath and bed after a wonderfully busy day. As I was driving a thought came into my head. *"Stop here."* I pulled over to the curb, but the traffic was zipping by.

I looked around and realized I had just passed a new food truck, the first Mexican Restaurant in the whole region.

"Lord, is that you talking? I'm not hungry. It's late. I recently talked to Max, the owner, and he may be closing now. Oh, okay. I'll turn around and go back."

I returned, parked, and walked under the little tent in front of the food truck. I was still wondering why I was there. Max greeted me from behind the counter. He and I traded small talk and then my phone rang on my WhatsApp that I use when in Brazil. It was a call from the US.

My daughter Cindy spoke, "Hi, mother. I need a favor. Could you give a message to Max for me? Will you have time before you leave Brazil?"

That was it!

"Okay. He is standing right here in front of me and you can talk to him yourself."

"Really? I can't believe that you are there at the *El Sombrero* restaurant at this time of night," she said.

"Oh, I'll tell you about it later."

I handed the phone to Max and sat down at the rustic table he had built himself. "Father, now I know why you sent me here at this very hour. Thank you for your special small voice."

Max handed the phone to me. He explained that she asked him for a copy of a photo he took years ago of her father playing chess. He said he would take the photo to his restaurant and I could pass by to get it before I traveled in just a few days.

I have been walking personally with the Lord since I was nine years old and I have learned to listen to His still small voice. But Father God still surprises me and I love Him for it!

"Follow the Cart"

One hot afternoon I was slowly driving up a steep city street behind a lady pushing a heavy cart. It was a common sight around town in Brazil.

People pile their homemade carts high with recycling material in order to exchange it for a few more Brazilian reais to make it through one more day.

But hers seemed especially heavy. She was really straining to push it up the hill. I could see an old four burner stove, scrap metal, besides the many plastic bags piled on top of things.

A thought came, *"follow the cart",* so I did. I was reminded that Jim always stopped to help the recycle peddlers because he felt at least they were working and not just begging. I loved to wait in the car to see their surprised look as he handed them money.

The lady and I arrived at the top of the incline about the same time. I pulled to the curb and got out of the car and walked toward her.

I called out to her, *"Senhora,* just a moment, please."

She stopped behind her cart and waited with her head down.

"I see you are a hard worker. I feel impressed to help you. I just filled up my car with gasohol, so I don't have much change."

She raised her head with a surprise look and said in Portuguese. *"Dona Shirley.* Are you in Brazil now?"

"Well, I am just visiting. I'm sorry but I don't recognize you," I said.

"You don't know me, but I know you. You took care of my grandchildren at Lar Nova Vida and I have always wanted to thank you."

"Really? How are your grandchildren doing today?" I asked.

"Oh, some are okay and others aren't. But you gave them opportunities when they were young to have a good education, and good health, and to have faith. And to make better decisions than some of them made. Uh, please come visit me."

I had received several invitations to visit homes those days, but that invitation touched me even more. Later that afternoon, Renata and I stopped in front of an alley way where she lived, among the items she had collected to recycle.

We visited, took photos, and hugged. Two grandmothers from different continents who want the best for their children and grandchildren.

Thank you, our Good Shepherd, for your small, whispering voice.

*****

Joaquim, really?

The lively group of Americans was to leave Brazil the next day and planned an afternoon of sightseeing. They were a mission group from the Rejoice Free Will Baptist in Owasso, Oklahoma. They had been in town for one week helping with Lar Nova Vida Children's Home and our churches in town, and Brazilian pastor Helio had rented a van to accommodate our visiting group to go on a sight-seeing trip.

As we were making plans, I felt an uneasiness about me going on the trip with them. I sifted through my feelings and a thought came in my head. *Joaquim. Joaquim?* Yes, for some reason I had an urgent need to visit him and Dona Julia that very afternoon. I couldn't visit with them later that night because we were going downtown to the city square for an open-air meeting. In the morning we would be packed to leave on our trip back to Oklahoma. Yes, I needed to go see them right then.

The group didn't question my explanation and they had a person with them who could help translate for them. Right before they left I went to *Joaquim's* house.

I clapped at his gate and his first words as he put his key in the gate's padlock confirmed my feelings. "I have been expecting you, Dona Shirley."

All afternoon was spent recalling the meetings on his small open front porch where the first services for the J. Candida FWB Church were held. He talked about his many children (19 totals of which 14 were still living) and grandchildren as a typical proud father would. About how he learned to read from reading the Bible.

I turned to Dona Julia and teased, "You know that today is Valentine's Day. You two need to celebrate, you know." (Brazil's Valentine's Day is in June.)

She smiled and said they had been married three times. "First we were married at the Justice of the Peace. The Catholic Church doesn't accept that without a church wedding, so, we got married there. Then we became evangelical Christians, so we had a nice wedding in our church. Married three times."

"And here we are 70 years later. Married and together," *Joaquim* said.

Finally, I said, "It is getting late and the group should be back soon for our open-air service downtown. I really need to go."

As we prayed, embraced and said our good-byes, tears came into my eyes during our last moments of holding each other.

After I returned to our *chacara,* I opened my journal and recorded the last delightful hours. A highlight of my trip.

But time passed and the group still hadn't arrived to go downtown for evangelism. Deacon Vicente drove up on his motorcycle with shocking news. "Have you heard the news?"

"No, what has happened?" I asked.

"Well, the group is down at the church. I'm sorry, but it is Brother *Joaquim.* After you left him this afternoon, he died. The American missionaries are down at the church preparing it to receive his casket. He wanted to have his wake at the church."

The family had called Pastor Helio on the cell. They returned immediately and asked him to come tell me. It was to be the first funeral at that church. Very few Brazilian wakes are held at a church. The body must be buried within 24 hours by Brazilian law, and the wake is usually in the home or at a small room near the cemetery.

I followed Vicente to the church and entered and sat on a bench with Dona Julia and some of her family. She said that after I left out their gate her husband told her that he was going to take a bath. She told him to not lock the bathroom door. She went to the kitchen and heard the water turn on in the shower and then a thud. She ran into the bathroom and found her husband fallen in the shower.

Since she couldn't find a pulse, she ran into the street and screamed for help.

When the ambulance arrived, he was already gone. He would have been 90 years old the next week. God invited him to celebrate early in heaven. She said she would cherish the happy afternoon we spent together. Oh, so would I!

The family asked me to share at the funeral the next day before we would catch our plane to the US. It was an honor for me, but the great joy was the fact that God whispered in my ear to go and visit with that sainted couple. The Good Shepherd knows the names of his sheep and they recognize His voice. God is full of surprises and I love Him for it.

*****

DRIPPING OIL

Another time I heard His whispering voice. I had not had as much experience at that time, so I doubted the voice for a few minutes, but God came through in a surprising way.

Our family was together for the holidays in Brazil trying to celebrate Christmas in 90-degree weather far from our relatives a continent away. I didn't want to spoil the good time so I didn't mention that I had noticed a lump. I waited a few days before I said anything and made an appointment with a Christian doctor in a neighboring city Ribeirao Preto.

"Dona Shirley, it is your gland. I have never seen one reach this size. I recommend you have surgery right away," Dr. Haroldo said. He recommended an immediate date.

"Oh, that is right during the Workers' Conference."

"Where is that?" he asked.

"Right here in Ribeirao Preto," I replied. I was in a lot of pain, but certainly wanted to attend that annual conference!

He reluctantly set it for noon on the last day of the meeting.

There was really no good time for something that with all the responsibilities of family and ministry, but my discomfort was going to limit activities anyway.

The conference was all I had hoped for. Most of the people there did not know about my surgery, so when I was asked to film the meeting, I complied. Some workers from neighboring country of Uruguay were on the program to sing.

A thought came when as I was filming, "Ask for prayer and anointing of oil."

"About the surgery?"

"As for prayer and anointing of oil," came the thought again.

"To be healed. Oh, how do I know if these are my own thoughts or from the Lord," I wrestled in my mind.

I continued filming.

God has healed me before, and he has allowed me to face the knife before. But I always had a time of preparation and scripture searching for a confirmation.

I continued to film.

"Lord, how can I know if these are my own thoughts? I want to believe that I am going to be healed BEFORE I ask for prayer. How can I know? I don't want to do something dumb. Oh, how I need a confirmation."

The Uruguayans were preparing their accordion and guitar for their first song in the last meeting before the closing fellowship lunch.

"Before we sing, I want to read a scripture that is appropriate for this moment," Pastor Mario began. "It is from Psalm 133."

"Behold, how good and how pleasant it is for brethren to dwell together in unity. It is like the precious ointment upon the head," he continued.

My eyes began to water as I looked through the lens of the camera. "Precious ointment?"

"Okay, Lord. I heard my confirmation and I will ask for prayer." I finally surrendered to His voice. During the last song I slipped out and whispered my request to missionary Bobby Poole.

Before closing, he called the pastors and workers up front to pray for me for my 'surgery in just a few moments'. I knew the prayer would be for healing, but I didn't say anything. He placed oil on my forehead and called on a young pastor Jose Laurito to pray for me. He was one of Jim's converts at the Jaboticabal Church where we were ministering and as he prayed, I felt God's power. A rush of tears. A warm sensation.

After the prayer I slipped back to the church office as quickly as possible to use the phone. My first thought was how embarrassing it was going to be to explain to the doctor, even with the fact of his being a Christian, that I was canceling surgery. Happily, the doctor was not in so I gave the nurse the message.

"Are you sure?" she asked.

"Oh, yes, I am very sure," I responded, I didn't check my lump immediately, however, because I knew that if it weren't gone already, it would be. Most of the pain was gone.

I told my surprised husband in the lunch line and Pastor Bobby and Pastor Jose. The next day the lump was gone!
*****

"the sheep <u>hear his voice</u>; and he calls his own sheep by name, and leads them out...he goes before them, and the sheep follow him; for <u>they know his voice</u>." John 10: 3,4

Chapter 11
Take Back Your Rainbow!

About 40 years ago in Brazil, we were beginning a Vacation Bible School week in the city of Araras, Sao Paulo. At that time, you couldn't buy a VBS set but you had to plan your own materials – theme, illustrated lessons and songs for each age, scripture posters, crafts, the closing service invitations, and certificates of participations. I prepared them and handed them out to our new Christian helpers.

One of the young teachers brought her teaching material on the story of Noah's ark and the great flood. She said in Portuguese, "I have a question about the end of the story. About the sign God put in the sky about His promise to His people. **About the rainbow**.

I nodded and waited for her to continue. "Well, since you are a foreigner, you may not know that the gays here in Brazil use the rainbow as their symbol. It doesn't seem right to leave out that beautiful part of the story, but I wanted to check with you first." At that time, we had flannel graph illustrations.

She was right that I was a foreigner and that I did not know.

I did know that already at that time Brazil, 40 years ago, was reported to have the largest number of open gays in the world. They had their part in the pagan yearly Carnival parades in the cities of Rio de Janeiro and of Sao Paulo. The media built up the scenes of the drag queens.

They had them as part of their daily soap opera and talk show interviews. But there were no manifestations and pressures for others who did believe in the Bible teachings.

I knew that the war between the "Angel of Light" and Christ followers was mixed with godly sounding vocabulary and subtle philosophy of the Father of Lies. And it has been going on since his prideful fall from heaven.

Love, Acceptance, and Tolerance

God is love so He created humans to love. To love friends, family, and an intimate partner. Beautiful, blessed by God's love. True love.

But Lucifer with all his splashy colors, mixes truth with lies. According to him, a new love definition must not take into consideration the God of the Bible. Also, tolerance and acceptance are not for others that insist on the Bible blueprint about life and love. If they only knew how much God loves them, has sacrificed for them, and wants to fill all the longing in their lives.

Some have never heard the true story of God's blueprint for life. Others have heard it, read it in the Bible, but because of friendships with those who reject it, they are confused and want to help their troubled friends. So they don't have the courage to shed light in the life of their troubled friends. Confusion may come when it is time to vote for a Bible believing public servant. Or whether to support other friends who think differently.

Love Them Enough

At the time of this conversation 40 years ago, I had made contacts with some young people who were confused about their identity and I had befriended them. But I had to love them enough. On my recent trips to Brazil I was in contact with two who are now adults.

One tall, handsome, young man approached me after a church service where our Brazilian foster son had preached. In Portugues he spoke, "You won't remember me but I am one of the children who lived by you. You would give us rides as we were walking to town. All the way to town you would talk about Jesus. He loved us and you loved us. He had plans for us. That we needed to study, stay healthy, and prepare for a great future. You gave us a lot of hope.

But some of our family would dress as girls at night and sneak out. We all lived in little cabins around our parents' homes. They never knew. And they were old, too. You told us that you would always help us and give us rides, but not when anyone was dressed in *"fantasia."* One of my brothers continued that life, but he committed suicide."

The young man had 100 more siblings adopted by a generous Spiritist couple.

He continued, "But I started going to a church that preached the Jesus of the Bible. The one you told us about. I surrendered to Jesus and was baptized. My wife and children are here tonight." He motioned for the waiting little group of four. We shared hugs and he thanked me for investing in their lives so long ago.

At another church service across town, another young man came and sat on the bench next to me. He had a nice singing voice. During the service the pastor welcomed me as a visitor that day and as a founding member of that church. The young man looked my way and smiled. After the service, he introduced himself and explained that he had been one of the little neighbor boys. He remembered that one day his mother had invited me to their home, after they had asked her many times, and he was the one she asked to take me around the interesting campus that housed many, many adopted children.

He reminded me that he had shown me one room where they had their Friday night séances. I remember a chill went over me that day. His parents taught them the practice of calling on 'good spirits' (demons, fallen angels) to possess them. They loved their children, I felt, but they only knew half-truths and could only pass that on to their children. Their children had all kinds of confusion. What a responsibility!

He shared, "After they died, we all lost our homes and scattered. Thankfully I found friends who took me to church. I was baptized and am a Christ follower. I am studying to be a male nurse at the hospital. I study really hard. Thank you for giving your time to some confused little boys." For those three months I was there, he sat by me in church.

Choices and Consequences

I taught the youngsters that God made us with the ability to make choices. He didn't create robots. Freedom of the will was important to God. But we don't choose the consequences. We teach the consequences of touching hot, dangerous things. About dangerous traffic. About poisonous insects and snakes. Science and experiences convince us that there are consequences.

One thing they didn't have to choose is if they are boys or girls. They are boys because God put XY in their genes. In their toes, elbows, and ears. There are over 30 trillion cells in their body with XY genes. Genes determine if you have straight or curly hair. Tall or short. Blue eyes or brown eyes. God had wonderful plans for them as boys. Maybe as husband, and fathers. Leaders.

If they decided to go against what God chose for them, there are consequences. God is all in for love, peace, and serving your fellowman. If you create your own doctrine and plans, in the long run you will have none of these permanently. He is against all ungodliness and unrighteousness. He loves you better than you love yourself.

Scriptures explain God's consequences. If you choose to ignore or change God's plan for men and women, sorry, but the consequences are still the same. "…vile passions. The women exchanged the natural use for what is against nature." "..the men, leaving the natural use of the women, burned in their lust for one another, men with men committing what is shameful, and receiving in themselves the penalty of their error which was due.

The bottom line is that if you choose to not go to heaven with me, my sorrow is heavy.

Back to Noah

So, back to Noah's Ark and the young teacher's dilemma 40 years ago. Do you already know what I told her?

"Take back your rainbow!"

"Let's not let Lucifer/Satan rob us of the beautiful symbol of truth and promise of God. The beautiful rainbow. God's promise. The dove that Noah sent out the window of the ark. God's symbol of our divine counselor and power. The Cross. God's symbol of sacrifice and love."

Forty years later as I see the rainbow used on tee-shirts, flags in businesses, and music concerts, even flaunted at our own White House in the past, my heart wants to say, 'You have taken my rainbow!'

These days, politicians may think that emphasizing it may get them more votes.

Businesses may think that government relations will be more favorable.

Television shows may count on bigger following.

Struggling musicians or famous artists may think it will give them a larger fan base.

Religious groups may think that rejecting Bible teaching will fill more pews and more offering plates.

Is It Worth the Cost?

Recently, a man who attended our church with his family had a high position in his company as an engineer for many years. He hired and trained workers. His salary for one month was more than I would receive in many years.

One day he entered the conference room for a leaders' meeting. What was different? The room was draped in rainbow flags. The speaker was a gay person explaining new company policies. My friend was surprised. The company had never taken a stand one way or another.

He talked to his boss about the meeting and told him he had no problem working with those with other preferences. He hired them and considered them to be fine workers. But as a Christian he could not promote it in his training sessions.

His boss told him that he would have to promote it or he could not continue with the company.

On his drive home that afternoon, he was troubled in his spirit and prayed for God's guidance. That evening he gathered his family together to explain the situation. The family agreed that he could not go against his Christian convictions. He should not. Even though he had no salary and had a family to support. He cooperated with others having opinions different from his, but they would not tolerate his unless he accepted theirs.

That same year the family opened a business that hires many people and God is still blessing Tony and family.

In 2019 it was reported that an American athlete was booed at an event. She declined a U.S. national team call-up in 2017 because she did not want to wear the team's LGBTQ Pride Month jerseys. She said, "I felt so convicted in my spirit that it wasn't my job to wear it." "I'm essentially giving up the one dream little girls dream about their entire life, and I'm saying no to (it)." She is a Christian.

Jaelene Hinkle is considered, by some, the top left back in the National Women's Soccer League. Her coach with the North Carolina Courage said that Hinkle was "the best left back in the league by a country mile" It is reported she had her strongest season yet in 2018 as she steamrolled them to a championship.

The coach and the captain of that year's U.S. team are openly gay. Two female members of the World cup are engaged to each other. The fullback and the goalkeeper. They receive applauses.

Recently the company our son has worked for years has started flying the rainbow flags.

Whose Pride?

Pride week. Pride month. Pride parade. Why am I not surprised with the chosen word 'pride'? Since I believe the Bible, I believe what is recorded about the Angel of Light, Lucifer, who rebelled in heaven. He wanted to be greater than God and because of his PRIDE, he was expelled from heaven with one third of the angels who fell with him.

Since his fall, he has gathered others who are deceived by his mixture of flashy colors, noble sounding platitudes, and false definitions of pride. He has sacrificed nothing for them. He is stealing many important years from the lives of our youth and adults. He is stealing their chance for a love relationship with Jesus who gave his life for them. Jesus is preparing a beautiful life after death. But Lucifer intends to steal that, too.

He must not steal God's promise symbol from us. TAKE BACK YOUR RAINBOW!!!

Chapter 12
The Last to Die
(No, to Suicide)

In Brazil we have a saying, *"A ultima que morre e' a Esperanca."* (The last to die is Hope.) And after hope dies, many times suicidal thoughts come.

Lying in bed recently as I was praying for friends contemplating suicide who reached out to me, I realized that I had made that same prayer with three that year. I remembered seven during my adult life who were close to me. Attempted suicides and successful suicides. Two who were successful in their suicidal attempts were reared in Christian homes. One had gone to a Bible College and the other was in the military. These two were brought to my attention after the fact. I was crushed. The other five I saw come out of their dark places and continued with their lives. This is a hard story to tell.

When I was a child, it was a subject whispered about and never spoken in front of children. If we did hear something, we didn't ask any questions because we weren't supposed to be listening!

But since then, I have had many questions. Why. Lord? Could I have done something to change their decision? Made a phone call? Written a card? Invited them over to my house? Invested more love and time and hope?

I know we need to pass on the Truth in the Word. There are resources to help care givers and families, but I want to share firsthand a story that took a friend and us down a dark path.

My husband met him in Welch College and our friendship has lasted over 50 years. My children and grandchildren called him "uncle". I received permission from his family to share this with you. We lived as residents of Brazil for 44 years and return there each year to serve as we are invited. He would stay from one month to six months with us while we were residents and then when we returned for short terms.

The first story began at our house in Brazil.

Last Chapter or Last Chance

One morning we loaded up the goodies into the car to take to the children of Lar Nova Vida. Pamela and I were to be there at nine a.m., so I went to check on my guest in his room. I hated to wake him up since I usually don't check on him so early, but I was compelled to go right then. Pamela went to use the email while I checked on him.

There was a handwritten sign on his door:

Shirley. Stop! Don't touch my body.

Go call Celso.

Call the coroner.

Thanks for all you and Jim have done for me.

"U"

Shocked, I read the sign again. Do I open the door? Do I follow his instructions? Yes, I'll call Celso. He was in the front house of our compound where I found Celso, his wife Renata, and Pamela. They greeted me with *bom dia* and smiles.

"Are you ready to go? I am almost finished here," Pam said. They didn't speak the same language but had become friends.

"Um, Celso, I need you to come with me to the guest room. It's very important," I told him in Portuguese.

"Okay. What is it?" he asked. They all stood waiting for my answer.

I explained about the note left on the door and that told me to call Celso. I invited the women to go, too. Renata is a nurse and Pamela a prayer warrior. It seemed that we would need both. On the way to his room, we were all praying in our own way to be prepared for what we would find.

As we stood in front of his door, I translated the sign. They were shocked. Pamela offered to go in first. Celso said, no, that the note told me to call him. I felt that if he were alive, he could hear us talking. I told them we would all go in together. The door was unlocked. Celso and I went in together and the women stood near the door.

He was alive, but he was in his blue recliner holding a small white handled knife over his wrist. He looked up and started telling me that it was already settled and not to waste time talking him out of it. He nodded his head toward papers he had written and laid at the foot of his bed near his chair. There was a note to me giving details of what to do with his things at our house in the US and separate letters to old friends and special people.

I knelt beside him and all the feelings I had, just poured out in tears for this man whom I had met the week of our wedding in 1963. We had worshipped God together. He was a friend and uncle to our children who he visited as they were growing up in Brazil. He was present when they married Brazilian mates in Brazil. Our grandchildren gave him hugs and he saved his peanuts and cookies for them from his plane trips. He went to their Grandparent's night at school and was there for their birthdays. He lived with us in Brazil and in Oklahoma and sat at our table. He was one of my husband's best friends and he was holding a knife!

"Oh, please don't do this. We love you. Our grandchildren love you so I can imagine how your grandchildren and great-grandchildren feel about you. You have many friends right here in Brazil who admire you."

"I am old and no good to anyone. What good is it to live when you are just trouble to people?" he asked.

"Aging is hard, and you are very limited, but you can eat, walk, and carry on a good conversation. You can play Mexican Train dominoes and Triominoes with us. You can recall things from the past and you are a great storyteller. We love having you around and we want to be the ones to help you."

He had lost most of his hearing and his osteoporosis was curving his neck pushing his chin almost to his chest. It was the rainy season and he hadn't been able to get out of his room for his daily swim. He was depressed.

"What keeps us going when we are ageing and feeble?

It is hope. We have hope that soon life will be over, and we have a better home and life waiting for us with the Lord. Hope that the 'valley of death' will end. The pain will end with no physical limitations. Loneliness will end. There is light at the end of the valley. The Shepherd is in the valley. Have you lost your hope? Let God decide your future."

In my hands was the letter he wrote to me. It is very personal, and I choose not to share all of it, but his opening lines were: "I have decided that my best course of action is to leave the Valley *of Tears* and launch into the wild blue yonder. Forgive me for doing this to you. I thank you and Jim for your love and friendship. Please express my thanks and love to the family…"

His 'valley' was not the valley the Psalmist wrote about. He could not see the Shepherd in the valley and lost hope.

He said, "I've talked to the Lord and he said that He and I will be floating out in the blue yonder somewhere. You can go with us if you want."

"Oh, no. I won't be floating out in space. I believe the promises in the word and I will be in heaven enjoying a perfect, eternal life. That is hope. I want you to be there with me and not floating in the unknown or experiencing eternal torment. There are two roads in life. It is our choice to make and God's promise to keep."

All the time I was wondering how to get him to let go of the knife. I told him that I wanted him to go over the papers of instructions he wanted me to read. He reached over and placed the knife at the foot of the bed and picked up the letters. Without turning away from him, I asked quietly in Portuguese for Celso to get the knife and leave with it. He nodded and sat down on the bed with me. He discreetly hid the knife in his hand and rose from the bed and left the room.

By the volume of the letters and instructions, I felt he must have been up all night preparing for everything. He could not be talked out of going through with his plans. Finally, I stood up.

"Listen, I am going right now to *Savanatur* tourist agency to get tickets out to the US tonight. The two of us can leave tonight. Celso will take us to the Sao Paulo airport."

"No, you are wasting your time and money. I am not going to return. You know I want my body to be cremated and I will only return in a jar of ashes. You can give them to my daughter. That way you can enjoy the rest of your visit here."

'Enjoy? It will ruin my trip here. I do not want you to talk like this. I am going right now to the tourist agency to change our tickets."

"No. It won't do any good. I will end it all today no matter what you say or do." My friend was getting upset with me.

I turned to the others standing in the doorway and told them I was going downtown to the tourist agency. By the time I got my documents and got ready to leave in the car, I saw him setting a bamboo porch chair out in the grass and he sat down in it. He had a blue handle steak knife in his hand!

By that time, Renata was crying, and she and Celso knelt on each side of him holding his wrists. He couldn't understand their Portuguese and they couldn't understand his English. He was really getting upset and wanted his hands free. They were determined to hold them until he surrendered the knife and we were all praying for guidance in what should be done.

He finally flipped the knife over in the grass and Celso picked it up. He was really exhausted by then, but got out of the chair with difficulty, went into his room. and slammed the door. The four of us were outside his door. Renata remembered that he had plenty of medicine to take in his room, but the door was locked. I went around to the window to see if we could break the glass to enter, but the metal shutters were closed. I met them again in front of his door.

"I'm still going to see about the tickets. Just let him be and maybe he will just sleep and wake up feeling better. We will keep praying. Prayer can penetrate walls that we can't pass through. We have done what we can. God is the God of miracles. We can pray protection for him that whatever he tries, will fail."

I drove the car to the automatic gate and while it was opening, I got out of the car and knelt prostrate on the rough driveway. We didn't have any solutions. A man without hope, locked in a room threatening to kill himself. My spirit groaned and the Holy Spirit took it to the throne of grace. I remember seeing through my tears a tiny leaf moving slowly on the cement between my hands, an ant carrying on as usual. That was what I must do. Press on. Carry on. Surrender it to God.

Downtown, I sat with the agents trying to change my tickets. There was nothing. Nothing until Sunday and it would be an extra $4,000 for him and no ticket for me to travel with him. I had to accept it and leave the rest to the Lord. I had surrendered, so I would wait.

When I returned to the *chacara,* they said it was all quiet in his room. They had called missionary Kimberly Johnson and she was there. I went in to make lunch for everyone. Press on. Make everything that my troubled guest likes. Rice and beans. Chicken and mashed potatoes, and salad. Kimberly called a couple of his friends who speak English. They had visited him in the US and always visited him at our house in Araras. Soon they showed up, too.

"Let's call him to have lunch and tell him the menu," I said. I knew they were thinking, is he alive?

We stood in front of his door and knocked. And knocked. And prayed. Finally, we heard the key rattle in his door. He just stood there and looked at all the people in the doorway. Pamela, Renata, Celso, Kimberly and me.

Pam said, "See how many friends you have? Shirley has lunch ready and she has made your favorite food. Come and eat with us."

He said weakly, "Okay. I guess I will go and eat." Those were his last words he would speak for several hours.

Yes, I was almost sure he had taken something. We needed to keep him awake. While the others were taking him to the kitchen, Renata checked his medicine. Some bottles were opened on the little table by the door and we didn't know how many were missing.

During the meal he kept falling asleep. The women cut up his food in tiny bites and tried to feed him. He would just hold the food in his mouth and fall asleep. Dr. Marina and her husband arrived and convinced him to go with them to see their little son. He agreed and they finally got him in their car. While they were gone, Renata cleaned out all the medicines, scissors, sharp objects left in his room and left them with me.

They stayed gone for a while and Dr. Marina brought him back with another friend, Dr. Camila. He seemed better but was still silent. Good, I thought, Dr. Camila is bossy, competent, and determined and he might just take it from her. She can help me with him.

He still hadn't said anything. Just kept his eyes closed and sat in the recliner. Was he still making plans? Or was he noticing his friends who wanted him to choose life? I told him I was going to take him to the hospital to get his blood pressure checked. He opened his eyes and looked at me. Dr. Camila backed me up and told him he would not have to wait since she was a doctor and could get him in immediately.

We helped him out of his recliner. He was very weak, and I unfolded his walker for him. Celso loaned him a clean, short sleeve shirt. (It was strange. He had arrived in Brazil with not one shirt! He had left one at our house from his last visit and I was washing it out each day. With the rainy season, we had not gone out to buy him more.)

We went to the hospital and Camila got us in right away. He saw Dr. Humberto who spoke English and was very patient with him. He checked his blood pressure, which was 140/90, and good for him. Then he asked him about overdosing on pills. We had brought the doctor the name of the medicine we thought he had taken. My friend broke his silence and told Dr. Humberto that he had taken ten pills.

The doctor explained that they wouldn't kill him but would make his stomach hurt and he would be very sleepy. We had already seen that! The doctor said he could connect him to fluids for about two hours at the hospital, but the best thing for him would be to put him to bed and let him sleep. When he woke up, his stomach would hurt, and he would think he was hungry. Feed him. He said to hide all pills from him. I asked him about the regular pills he takes, and the doctor said he could go off all of them for a while

I got the car and drove around to the emergency entrance where Dr. Camila and he were waiting. We put him in the front seat and as I was folding up the walker, she whispered that he said he wanted some salad and a sandwich. Great, and off we went to get him something to eat.

He ate most of his food in silence. He gave his milkshake to Camila; she was so helpful and so competent. I thanked her and the Lord as we parted at the restaurant. She marked to take him out to eat the next day.

When we arrived back home, he was calm and leaned back in his recliner and went to sleep. While he was asleep, I went downtown to the telephone company and made an international call to Jim, my husband, who was in Oklahoma. He said there wasn't much he could do but had been praying about what should be done.

That night Jim contacted Celso by skype (the first night they had used it) and said that he would be leaving Oklahoma the next day, Friday, and would be traveling back with Richard on American Airlines on Monday. Jim had called his daughter and she thought it would be good for him to travel back with Jim.

After I got back to the *chacara,* he woke up and I made him some hot milk and coffee. I helped him get to bed and left his door without a key to lock it. I felt sad but thankful.

The next day he was talking and asking about Jim. It seems that he didn't remember many things about the day before.

Jim arrived Saturday after traveling all night, and we went through the weekend preparing for the return trip. My guest friend seemed to perk up after Jim arrived.

On the flight back to Oklahoma, Jim said he shared that since I never checked on him that early in the morning he thought it "would all be over by the time I returned and found his sign." Also, he explained why he put the chair in the grass on the second attempt to "avoid the messy bloody situation". So, he does think about that day. I know I do.

But unhappily we faced it together again.

Heat Wave with Depression Cloud

It was over 100 degrees F. on an Oklahoma summer day as I pulled into our driveway and pressed the control to open the garage door. What? There in the hot garage he was sitting in his motorized wheelchair in my parking place with his head hanging down. I stopped the car in the middle of the driveway and helped the two granddaughters, Bianca and Isabela, get out of the car. The girls greeted their elderly 'uncle' seated in the chair, but he didn't respond. They entered the house through the very hot garage, and I was glad they didn't asked questions.

I walked by his chair and asked, "Hey, does your scooter chair still run okay?"

He opened his eyes.

"Yes, it still does okay." At least his voice sounded pretty normal.

"Remember, you have the other smaller chair if you want to drive in the neighborhood when it gets cooler. Its battery is good, too, and may be easier to handle."

Why was he just sitting in that terribly hot garage by himself? Surely he wasn't thinking about going somewhere now. Jim's old Lincoln car was gone.

Before arriving, I had promised the girls that we would cut the cold cantaloupe in the refrigerator when we got home. They reminded me that I had already promised a fruit milkshake. While I was cutting the cantaloupe at the sink, he came into the kitchen and passed behind me. Only later did I realize what he was doing.

"Do you want some cold fruit?" I asked. Thankful that he had entered our cool house.

"Humm, maybe I'll take some later." He left the kitchen and passed through the living room.

Jim came in about that time. I started mixing the fruit shake in the noisy blender.

"Hi. Was the garage door up? I left it up because he was sitting in his scooter chair out there in the terrible heat."

Jim said he thought it was down. I went to the door and looked into the garage. The garage door was closed, and he was sitting out there again. The shake was ready, so I went back to the kitchen to prepare him a glass and took it to the garage. He didn't look up at me. He had a knife to his left wrist and blood was running on each side and around his wrist. Once again!

"Oh, don't do that. Don't. Here is some shake that you like. Drink it. It's' very cold." I took the knife from his hand and handed him the glass.

He took the glass and drank the shake. What do you say to a person that has lost all hope? I told him he must have hope and faith and he could look forward to a better life, but that time was not for us to decide.

"Oh, it would take you a long time to bleed out. Please don't do this," I pleaded.

He said, "You wouldn't think a person's hide would be that tough. If I cut it the right way, it will bleed more and faster."

"I know it is terrible to lose your strength and have to be dependent more and more. We are here to help you. We want to help you."

He bowed his head, "I'm no good this way. I'm no good to myself or to anybody else."

Bianca opened the garage door and looked in. I slowly hid the bloody knife behind my back. She asked a question and I answered it. She looked over the situation with the curiosity of a ten year old and then left.

"Last week before we went to Texas, you said you wanted to go to Kentucky to visit friends. As soon as we meet our obligations, we'll make plans to take you. Jim has relatives there, too."

"I don't need to go anywhere. I'm no good this way."

"Listen, it is very hot in here. I'm going to take these things back into the kitchen." When I passed Jim at the computer, I showed him the bloody knife. He knew what it meant.

I poured my shake into a little glass pitcher and took it to the garage to offer him.

"No, I don't want anymore." He was still sitting in the chair staring at the floor. I knew that it doesn't do any good to pressure him, so I went back into the house and prayed. And prayed.

Jim and I talked a while and Jim shared that our friend had been talking about some strange things that "made sense now." We heard the door from the garage open and the alarm beeped. He was coming in and slowly went down the hall to his room.

Jim asked me what I thought he should do. I wet a clean cloth with cold water and told Jim to take it to put over the cut on the wrist. By now he was in his room. Jim took it to him.

Jim said that when he gave him the wet cloth, he asked, "Are we still going to play games tonight, Jim?"

Jim told him we would play games right after we returned home from prayer meeting. I wondered if we should leave him alone, but Jim said we couldn't watch him every minute and must go on with our duties. All during the ride to church, during the meeting, and on the way home, a 'chill' hit me as I remembered the knife on his arm. Even after I went to bed I remembered the scene again and my sadness was heavy. (I knew I had to get it out of my mind, so I put it down on paper. It helped.)

As soon as we entered the house from prayer meeting, Jim went to his room and told him to come eat a snack and then we would play games. He ate at the table and stayed there while we set up 'Triominoes".

Every night we played it or Mexican Train with dominoes. The last two nights he had won games.

That night he won the last game.

I wondered what he was thinking when he returned to his room. There were spirits of depression and suicide who hover over to rob, kill, and destroy. I prayed God would give us words to encourage him by. Through the name and blood of Jesus Christ he could resist them, and we prayed that he would allow the sweet peace of the Holy Spirit to take control.

He could win again, but he couldn't do it alone.

The next day our son Kemper and I prayed in the powerful name of Jesus and through His blood that the hovering spirits of depression and suicide would leave our house. That the Holy Spirit in all His plenitude (fullness) would fill our house and lives with glorious peace.

Well, our friend woke and said he was feeling better. He went through his regular routine with a pleasant attitude. It was partly cloudy and not quite so hot. All day I had be praying about talking to him about his spiritual condition. All afternoon I was not feeling well but didn't want to mention it. If it were the old enemy trying to take away my chance to talk, I would just resist.

That chance came after two games of dominoes, which he won. He and Jim bantered back and forth and joked about the game for a few minutes as we cleared away the game and put the table back to order. I asked him to wait a few minutes so that we could talk. Jim left us alone.

The time had come. I sat down at the table with him.

"When we first met, you were a Bible teacher and church leader. We worked together with you and your family and became great friends. Through the years, things changed. You are super intelligent and very curious to discover new things, so you opened up to other philosophies, religious books, and world religions. You even started your own religion and taught that *love* was the answer to everything. And finally, the New Age movement."

He was looking straight at me with his hand cupped behind his right ear. I hoped he was hearing me.

"But those religions are not enough for you right now. They are not giving you hope and strength to face the changes in your life. Where are they when you need them?"

He said, "Most of the time I have a positive attitude about life. I have always had a positive attitude until now."

"I believe," tapping my chest, "personally believe that there exist hovering spirits that try to defeat us. Last night Kemper and I prayed in the name of Jesus and through the powerful blood of Jesus that any spirit of depression, of suicide, of confusion would be cast out of our house. I want to know if you will accept prayer for yourself to be free of these thoughts and to have peace in the Lord."

"Some days you are positive and converse and other days you are depressed and think about suicide. These negative spirits seem to come and go, and they need to know that they are not welcome!"

"I am a Christian now and have left all those other things. I feel I will go to heaven when I die," he said.

I reached for his hand. "Good. I am so glad. That is a great hope."

"Then those comments you once made that you weren't going to heaven, but you are going to just be floating out in space someplace, have changed now?" I asked.

"Right, because I didn't want to go to a place where we do nothing. I would be bored. But you said the Bible taught we would be serving in heaven," he answered.

"Oh, I believe that there will be many things to do and a structure of satisfying things to do and accomplish and that we will be totally fulfilled. Maybe according to our interests and talents here we will be matched with some service up there."

"Who knows? There will be gardens, buildings, music, to participate in and galaxies to learn about. It is beyond our imagination and understanding what God has prepared for us."

"Some people think it will be an eternal church service. I imagine it will be a time of many activities, but when we are called to time of worship, it will be a joyful experience. I don't believe we will hesitate but will gladly join in with people from all over the world who have surrendered to His love and will," I shared.

At that moment I took his hand and felt I should share about my elderly parents. I told him about my father who was in a wheelchair for the last years of his life. It was very difficult for him, but he had a good attitude and never lost his faith to the end. For two years after an unsuccessful knee surgery he carried fever in his body and was confined to a wheelchair. He was a strong, healthy man but dependent on others. He was a contractor as well as a preacher. He preached from his wheelchair at times

One night he fell from his unlocked wheelchair as he stretched to lock a door. His leg was broken but not his spirit.

However, the hospital gave him medicine he was allergic to and his body closed down. It killed him. It was a blow to all of us. It was difficult, but maybe it was part of God's mercy that kept him from suffering longer.

Our mother as a pastor's wife cared for many people, but because of heart attacks and strokes she was bedfast for six years. She couldn't sit up, feed or dress herself, and could not talk. However, when we five daughters gathered around her bed and sang, she could sing quietly with us. Forming words and harmonizing with her alto voice! Some of the nurses had never heard her say a word. Only tuh-tuh-tuh-tuh. Although most of her senses were locked inside her, she drew deeply from her faith in Christ for 80 of her 92 years and sang praises to Him."

I told him we had put up rails and other things to help his mobility. Also, if he reached the point he needed the walker or wheelchair constantly, we would adapt. We would help him and wanted to help him. He just needed to keep hope and faith in Him.

"I don't think you liked it, but when I put the knife to my arm yesterday, I thought it was for the best. Today I feel different. I don't think I'll need the rails much and I still do pretty well if I use my walker."

By this time, we were walking down the hall toward his room. I felt a relief that a burden had been lifted and I had great news to pass on to his children.

He could remember that he was not alone.

The Last Chapter

In his room was the autobiography of his life that he asked me to help him write. Over one hundred pages of adventures of a little Kentucky boy who grew up to serve in World War II, to receive his doctorate, and to serve on national committees for the good of the handicapped community. He was a father, grandfather, and a friend to many, many people. He was married to his red-haired sweetheart who was a teacher and daughter of a Free Will Baptist preacher.

He was a university professor and had traveled to all the continents of the world and had many tales to tell. But the last chapter was never written in his autobiography.

Let me write it now.

He contracted pneumonia at the age of 88, went to the hospital, and then to a rehab home to regain the use of his legs before he could return to our house. It was in a nearby city and Jim visited him every day and I on most days.

His daughter and granddaughter came to visit him and brought posters for his room of famous themes, just like he enjoyed.

One day when I was visiting he asked, "Is my room near a door?"

"Yes, it is. Not the front door, but it is at the end of this hallway."

"I am ready to go home," he said from his bed.

"Well, the recliner is yours so we will have to get Rodrigo to come in his truck. He can't tonight."

"Oh, they said I can't go to your house until I can walk by myself again."

"Okay, let's work on that so you can get to that point," I offered. But each day he got weaker.

One day Jim went by himself for his daily visit to our dear friend in the next city. He had practically stopped eating and stayed in bed most of the time. Jim had taken him his favorite milkshake, but he didn't want to try any and lay back down. Since Jim went there every day, he had made several friends. He stepped out into the hall to visit with others living there in treatment.

When he returned to our friend's bed, he was so still Jim checked his breathing. Quickly he called the nurses to check him. They immediately started reviving him but Jim stopped them reminding them of the signed orders that the 88 year old patient had left. It was a comfort for Jim to know that he was alive those first moments when he arrived. He didn't leave this world without a devoted friend present.

As the neighboring patients saw what was happening, they remarked, "He is lucky. He gets to leave."

Yes, he was fortunate that he left his home going date up to the Lord and now he knows firsthand what God has prepared for all of us in heaven.

*****

Chapter 13
This and That

For How Long, Lord?

Were you amazed or shocked by these stories of God-miracles of the impossible?

We the common, ordinary factors become participants with an extraordinary God. So, we don't need to produce solutions and answers to difficult situations or to everyday needs, because God is ready and powerful to take care of His children. On my yearly mission trips, I see God use people who are willing to partner with Him to see the impossible.

I don't know if Apostle Paul and his co-missionaries had people to help finance their missionary trips like I have had. Maybe some of the same New Testament women who helped Jesus and His disciples helped them. But one day Paul said to Barnabas, "Let us go again and visit our brethren in every city where we have preached the word of the Lord." And we know he did just that. (Acts 15:36)

Each year I have been able to return to our beloved people in Brazil where we have preached the word of the Lord since 1965. (We arrived in 1964 but couldn't communicate in Portuguese until 1965. Well, sort of using 'baby talk'.) The places in general have undergone many changes. More businesses, urbanization, and population explosion have given an unfamiliar face to the familiar past of last year.

I noticed there were a few more air conditioner window units. You could close the windows to protect from mosquitos if you had one. But we still bought lots of regular fans for the children's homes and there was no A.C. where we stayed.

But the people? Their faces change as nature changes them with age. If you observe carefully, you see some gospel seed fell by the wayside, and others withered away for lack of depth. But others kept faithful and are bringing forth a great harvest. The healthy churches starting other churches is a tribute to those who labored and those who have sponsored the laborers.

I noticed that their meetings start right on time now, but still some of the folks arrive past time for them to begin. However, there is no certain time to finish and they gladly meet several times a week.

At prayer meetings they pray. Long, heart felt prayers by many participants. On their knees, sitting, or standing up. They report on the answered prayers and add more to the list. Things happen. Their custom is to see the New Year in on their knees while the city is celebrating with fireworks. Then there is a midnight feast together with the church family for a few hours. Prayers continue through the new year.

They still are in love with the Word. New Christians, mature Christians, and non-Christian friends will meet weekly for special courses and then proudly receive a certificate of study in a special "graduation" ceremony with photos and congratulations. Each time I visit I learn from my Brazilian friends and always hope to return.

But they are not immune to envying, grudges, and ill will toward one another as they learn to live and work as a body. I am amazed at how their pastors deal wisely and compassionately with each situation and how there is spiritual growth for everyone involved. For the battle is not with each other, but against Satan who wants to implode the whole work of the Holy Spirit who is building God's Kingdom.

Do we stay in the battle with such faith that Satan will be worried about us? Us? Ordinary and common us? Oh, yes!

When we depend totally on our Holy Spirit to be our sufficiency and we turn loose of our independence, we become partners with a miracle working God. I say we don't need to struggle in fear of defeat for we will always see Jesus win the battles over the power of darkness. Faith is a small word and is even smaller in Portuguese. Just two letters. *FE'*. But it results in powerful answers.

I enjoy watching athletic students at Randall University as they go in and out of the classroom, to chapel meetings, as they go in and out of gymnasiums, and on and off the playing fields. Their coaches make sure they stay in good physical shape with daily training. They have the physical power they need.

But it is interesting to see the arrival of the referees. They don't need to have the same physical power of the players because they have the authoritative power of the whistle and of the yellow and red flags.

Dear reader, we don't need to have the strength enough to combat the Father of Lies, because we have the authority of the Mighty Father God to call the shots.

That is better than a whistle and yellow and red flags. We can call upon the name and blood of Jesus Christ, the Son of God! It never fails.

We can ask as Isaiah asked, for how long? Remember to tell your friends and family, this generation, what God has done for you. It doesn't have to be great stories. We are stewards of the stories God is doing today. Tell your stories of everyday things and give God the glory.

Missionary/professor Laura Belle Barnard taught that to tell the gospel is binding upon all who have accepted God's salvation. Those disciples who heard the commission from the lips of the Savior could not have completed the task without the enlistment of succeeding generations. That included all of us. There has never been a repeal of this command. No amendment.

The Bible says, "And this gospel of the kingdom shall be preached in all the world for a witness unto all nations; and then shall the end come." (Matthew 23:14) The Holy Spirit is gathering out "a people for His name" to be the Bride of Christ.

One day missionaries, their sponsors, all Christ followers who have won souls to Him, will witness a scene the Bible describes as "a great multitude , which no man could number, of all nations, and kindreds, and people, and tongues, stood before the throne, and before the Lamb, clothed with white robes, and palms in their hands." (Rev. 7:9) Glory!

Are you ready for a prayer journey with expectancy to carry out that command? It is humbling and life changing. Prayer works and makes a difference. Just do it. It's true!

Jim's last Christmas - 2016

Jim's last birthday - January 2017

Jim's last Sermons

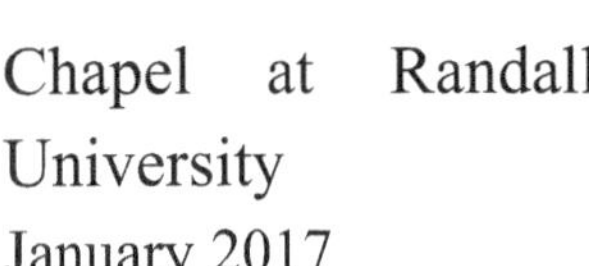

Chapel at Randall University
January 2017

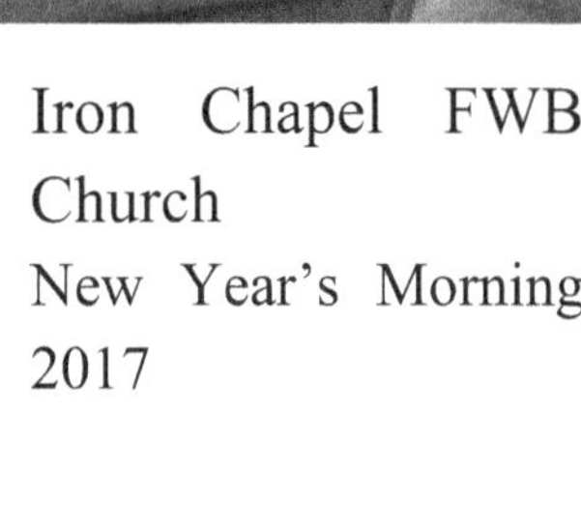

Iron Chapel FWB Church
New Year's Morning 2017

Dibble FWB Church
Communion and feet washing
New Year's Evening 2017

Johnny, Marco, and Rod

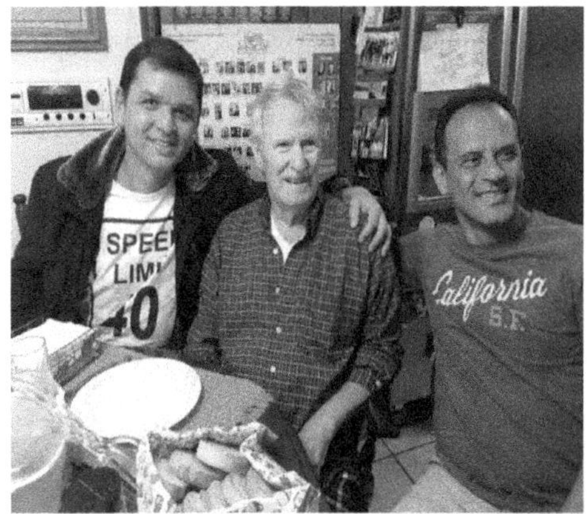

Last day visits with friends from Brazil

Sergio and Pastor Jose

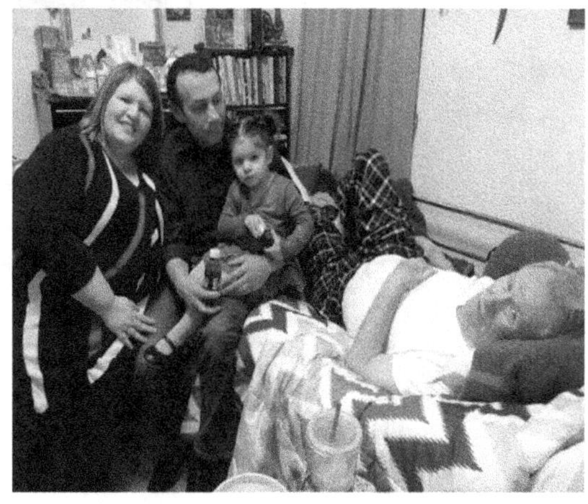

Kimberly, Henrique, and Lynli

A Young Mother's Story

Baby Ana
"Pronounced dead after birth"

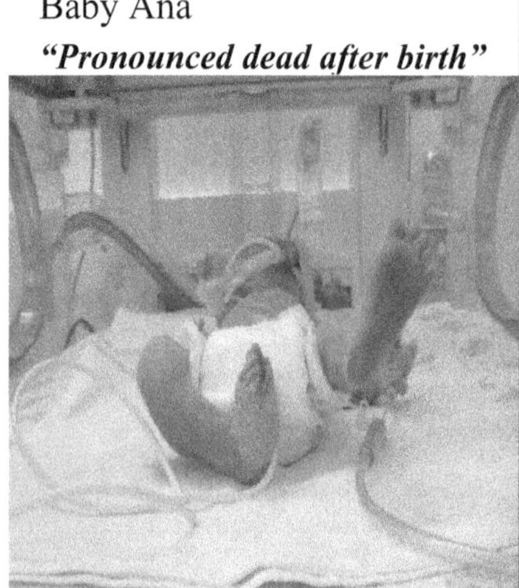

Ana Carolina today
"A testimony of a miracle"

Word Whispers

Step Outside   **"Stop Here"**

""Follow that Cart"

"Jim playing chess"

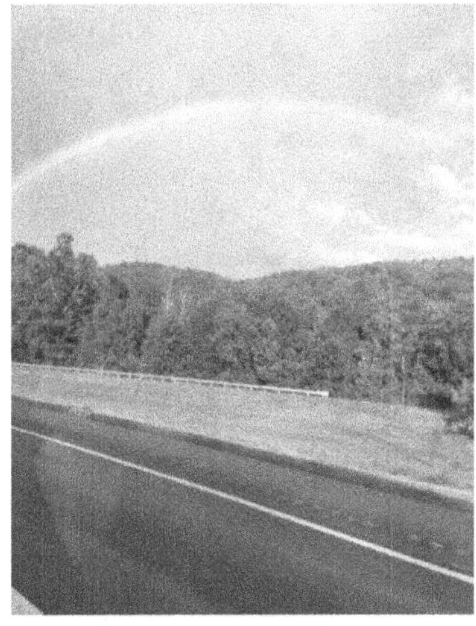

"Take Back Your Rainbow"

Home Sweet Home – *Lar Doce Lar*

Araras, SP
Brazil, SA

Moore,
Oklahoma
USA

Appendix
This and That by Others

1. Jim's sister, Judy Combs Puckett, wrote the following paper two weeks after he was diagnosed with cancer and had only a short time to remain on this earth. The following excerpt is used with her permission.

Three Men of God
By Judy Combs Puckett

In early October 2016, I learned that my brother-in-law Ed Cook was retiring from his pastoral ministry, which began 58 years ago. I began to think back about those early years when he and my sister Nancy first married. He and Nancy invited his best friend and roommate Jim Puckett (my husband) for a visit, and we began dating. The three of them were also classmates of my brother Jim Combs and his wife Shirley Roberts at Free Will Baptist Bible College (re-named Welch College) in Nashville, Tennessee, which is how the lives of these three preachers and their wives connected and began to be intertwined.

At that time, we did not know that my brother Jim Combs had cancer, a diagnosis he received just two weeks ago today. His diagnosis confirmed to me that the Lord inspired me to capture this history in written form before it escaped my mind.

The term "man of God" has been revered and reserved for only the most dedicated among us, first used in the Bible to designate the Old Testament prophets. Eventually it became a more generic term to refer to anyone in ministry. We seldom use or hear it today, though there are many who qualify.

Without a doubt, several of my family and close friends exemplify the term. Among our families, it is not uncommon to have ministers. There are eight ordained ministers on my side of the family, seven of whom are still living. My father was the first in his family. Several others are not ordained but are working in ministry positions.

My husband's family has a similar heritage going all the way back to his great-great grandfather. There are seven ordained ministers, four of them still living.

With this many ministers it is easy to take their work and dedication for granted. These men have impacted literally thousands of lives, scores of churches, and numerous cities and towns during their 50-plus years of ministry each. Though they came from three different states, their lives intersected as classmates, roommates, and friends in college. And their shared ministry and family connection has kept them close for nearly 60 years.

James Kemper Combs

My brother Jim Combs grew up in our hometown of Crab Orchard, West Virginia. Jimmy Kemper, as he was known, answered the call to preach in his late teens during the mid-1950s while serving in the navy. A few years later at Free Will Baptist Bible College he answered the call to missions. It was there he met his wife Shirley Roberts, a fellow mission student. After graduation, he and Shirley married and later moved to Brazil where they entered language study to learn Portuguese and served as Free Will Baptist missionaries in Brazil from 1964 to 2008. They spent a few of those years as missionaries–in-residence, as professors, and director of the mission's department at Hillsdale College (now Randall University) in Moore, Oklahoma, pastored a church in Dibble, and served as chaplain for the Oklahoma prison system.

In Brazil he served in several cities in the states of Sao Paulo and Santa Catarina. In the US he served in the states of Tennessee, Ohio, and Oklahoma. In 2004 Jim and Shirley Combs officially retired from Free Will Baptist Foreign Missions (re-named International Missions) and continued in Brazil in ministry until they moved back to the US from Brazil in 2008 to be near their children and six grandchildren. They continue to be involved in raising funds and awareness for Lar Nova Vida and made yearly trips back to Brazil to serve the Children's homes and churches.

Edward Cook

My brother-in-law Ed Cook, a native of St. Louis, Missouri, answered the call to preach during the early-1960s while attending Free Will Baptist Bible College. Ed also met his future wife, my sister Nancy Combs, in Nashville. They married while still students, and Ed followed Jim Combs as pastor of Stoney Point FWB near Nashville. After graduation in 1963, Ed and Nancy moved to Miami, Florida, to pastor Golden Glades Church, and they have continued to serve in the pastoral ministry since that time. They served in the states of Tennessee, Florida, Oklahoma, Kentucky, Arkansas, and North Carolina. In October 2016, Ed Cook resigned from the Heritage FWB Church in Ashland, Kentucky and retired on December 31, 2016.

James Puckett

My husband, Jim Puckett answered the call to preach during the late-1950s while still a teenager in Pine Bluff, Arkansas. He also studied at FWBBC, where one of the first students he met was his good friend and eventual roommate Ed Cook, Jim and I also met during his days as a student in Nashville, while I was still in high school. We would later reconnect in Florida where he had moved after graduating in 1962. During the summers before and after his senior year, he served as pastoral intern for FWB churches in Raleigh, North Carolina and Miami, Florida. In the fall of 1963 Jim began serving as minister of music and youth at Wesconnett FWB Church in Jacksonville, Florida, under the leadership of his former pastor and mentor Elro Driggers. We married in 1965 and served in Jacksonville as associate and interim pastor for one year before moving to south Florida to begin his pastoral ministry at Deerfield Beach.

Jim's pastoral ministry continued until 1999 when he resigned to become Director of Missions for Oklahoma Free Will Baptist. He served as State Mission Director until 2007 and has continued to serve as interim pastor of various churches and to preach intermittently for vacationing pastors. He is now working in real estate investment – buying, renovating and re-selling homes – but continues to help churches when needed.

It's easy to see that I am very proud of these three preachers. I realize I am biased when it comes to three guy who are so near to my heart, but I can truthfully say that they are among the finest men I know. In all their ministry accomplishments, I didn't mention that each has been a wonderful father and grandfather who have lived as examples to their families. Their work, character, and love for the Lord, for the work of ministry, and for people is an example to follow.

I thank the Lord for the privilege of being associated with each of these men of God.

(Note: James Kemper Combs moved his address to heaven on February 7, 2017, and his life was celebrated at Randall University in Oklahoma on February 11th with about 500 family and friends present)

2. This tribute from Dr. Mary Holland was read by her husband, Curt Holland, at the home going celebration of Jim Combs on February 11th, 20217 at Randall University in Moore, Oklahoma.

Mary's Tribute

There is so much to be said about this man who came from Crab Orchard, West Virginia; a place Jim was always proud to call home. His fond memories of his childhood and life with a big family always brought good stories, a song or two, and a twinkle in his eye. Some knew him as a boy, and I can only imagine his quick wit, adventurous spirit was nurtured in his childhood in the hills of West Virginia.

He was also a US navy man. This experience undoubtedly shaped his love for his own country, and he enjoyed the freedoms we are blessed with. But I imagine it influenced how he organized himself, how the thought about life and how it should be enjoyed in simplicity.

Jim was known by so many names: husband, *bem, pai,* dad, *tio,* uncle, granddad, *vovo,* friend, *amigo,* querido, Pastor, teacher, brother, *irmao, filho,* son. All names endearing but each represented a relationship he had developed with those who called him by these names.

He held three citizenships and honored all three well; America, Brazil, and his newest and final residence: heaven. With that being said, the amount of people he knew and relationships he built grew exponentially throughout his 79 years on this earth. We will all miss Jim Combs at different capacities. My heart aches for his children and grandchildren who knew they had one-of-a kind of father and grandfather. To have been loved so well by Jim --who they will miss severely. His extended family will also grieve for the little boy from WV who grew up and followed the leading of his Savior.

For the rest of us, adopted by Jim, if you will, we grieve too. All of us here have had our feet under his table, have ridden in his Kombi Volks Van, spent the night or two at his house, eaten from his churrasco, heard him preach the Word, felt his hand on your shoulder as he prayed over you, heard one of his stories, were encouraged by his words, lost to him in Chess, attended a field council meeting, heard him laugh at his own jokes, seen him cry, watched him love on children, hosted your team, was shepherd by him, heard his impeccable Portuguese, or watched a soccer game,. All of us felt validated because he simply cared and loved all people unconditionally.

The one who I have not mentioned because her loss is too great for me to comprehend is Jim's beloved Shirley. To be honest, it has been Jim & Shirley for so long, it will be hard for us to say just Shirley. Their devotion and love for one another has always been fueled by their passion and love for Jesus. In fact, it is impossible to celebrate the life of Jim Combs without celebrating the life of Shirley Combs. Two selfless people who would do anything to show the love of Christ and further His kingdom. Today, I honor with you our beloved, *querido* Jim Combs. May we live in submission to the Christ he served and loved, and may our goal be to love people in the way Christ loved people through Jim and Shirley Combs. Ate' logo our Jim Combs.

3. Our granddaughter wrote some songs about her grandfather, Jim Combs, during her grieving days. She sang this first song to him at the hospital with her guitar and wrote the second after he went to glory. These lyrics I share with her permission

 **I DON'T WANNA LOSE YOU** 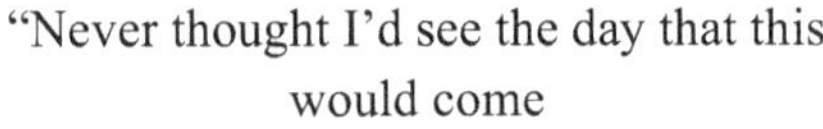
"Never thought I'd see the day that this
would come
Oh, no.
I'm losing control.
I don't wanna think about this life without you.
Oh, no.
Please don't go.
(Chorus)
They tell me to stay strong
But I don't wanna lose you.
They tell me it's alright
But I don't wanna lose you.
Just another song.
Just another story.
Let's try to stop the time
and create another memory.
I don't wanna lose you.
I don't wanna lose you.

And I wish I could ask God to keep you here
Oh, no.
It's just too soon.
But I know when He calls you just have to go.
Oh, no.
What will I do?
(Written by Julia Marita (Combs) de Aquino)

4. Julia wrote this song a short while after her grandfather passed on to glory. All of us need a grieving time but cannot put our feelings to music like she did.

 **WITHOUT YOU** 

I wanna see you again.
It's not the same without you.
I look back on the moments
We had with you.

When we would sit and
You'd tell us stories
About the good old days.
I can't believe that
You're gone forever
And now it won't be the same.
(Chorus)
Without you, you, you.
Without you, you, you.
Without you, you, you,
Without you.

I know you're where you belong
And I know you're smiling down
But right now it's hard
To think about. (Chorus)

And now I know

That you are in a better place
So I can't help
But think about the better days.

When we will sit and
You'll tell us stories
About the good old days.
One thing I know is
One day in heaven
It'll all be the same.
I'll be with you, you, you.
Be with you, you, you.
Be with you, you, you.
I'll be with you (2X)
(Written by Julia Marita (Combs) de Aquino)

5. Both of the following were written November 29, 2002, by my niece Elisabeth Shivers Collett for her mother and her aunts about her grandmother, Lucy Marie Laughlin Roberts. (My mother) It is written as if her grandmother were talking to us.

My Name Is Marie

I am here because I can no longer care for myself.

- Before arriving here, I was more than a patient with a diagnosis, treatment plan and room number.
- I had a life, a home and a family. I had hobbies, interests and skills. I had hopes, dreams and goals.
- All that I lived and worked for has been sold, given away or passed on to someone who can't quite appreciate it the way I did.
- When you care for me, remember:

My name is Marie.
I used to be just like you.
Someday…You could be just like me., Marie

6. Remember Me, Before I Forgot You

Please forgive me if I have forgotten you.

Remember how much I loved you before my memories became lost in the   dark shadows of my mind.

Please be patient with me if I am unkind and will not cooperate.

Remember that I am only frustrated, confused, and frightened.

This world that I exist in is just as unfamiliar to me as it is to you.

Please be brave and strong and don't let me walk through it alone.

Kiss my face and hold my hand.

The shell you see may not respond, but my heart will know.

My heart has not faded with my mind.

It is only unable to express itself.

Look beyond the stranger I have become.

Remember who I was…

Before I forgot who you are.

7. Lyndon Ray Berglan has given me permission to share his poem on prayer. He says every need is a new prayer, an opportunity to grow closer to the Lord, and that we may not recognize God's miracles.

GOD OF OPPORTUNITIES
By Lyndon Ray Berglan
My God answers prayer.
Every need is a new prayer,
A new opportunity to grow closer to Him,
To become stronger, wiser, kinder,
And a little more patient
With others facing their own opportunities.

Opportunities are not convenient.
They don't come when I am ready.
They make me ready for what comes.
Opportunities don't save me
From the consequences of my actions.
They open the door to correct my mistakes today
And teach me to make better choices tomorrow.
My God is not a God of convenience

Who gives me what I want when I want.
What kind of Father would that be?
He is a God of opportunities
Who gives me what I really need.
It is easy to overlook His miracles
When they arrive as opportunities
That require me to grow so I can receive.

My God is here, there, and everywhere
I need Him to be.
He is always with me, supporting me, encouraging me
I need Him to be.
Today I am a lump of coal
But God sees a diamond in the making,
So, He gives me opportunities.
#poetry (c.) Lyndon Berglan

8.   I CANNOT WAIT
By Ed Seabough

Lord, you placed me in this world
Of time and space and missiles hurled,
With eyes I've seen the Ghetto Gloom,
With ears I've heard the sonic boom,
And man cry out for breathing room.
Lord, you asked for all my life
In Healing Hurts and ending strife,
With mind to always seek the truth,
With voice to always speak the truth,
And life to manifest Christ's worth.
Lord, I give my life to you,
My Time, my talents, each day new.
With faith to witness to your plan,
With hope to gladly take my stand,
And love to minister to man.

I cannot wait, I cannot wait!
Here is my life, I want to live it.
Here is my life, I want to give it.
Serving my fellowman, doing the Will of God.

They Must be Sought
By Rita Jane Wilson

The lost will not seek, they must be sought.
The lost will not come; they must be brought.
The lost will not learn, they must be taught.
Lord, help me to do my part!

My talented niece Deborah Sue Hale was born on Christmas day and has grown into a compassionate member of our family. While being a teacher with many talents, she has entertained our family with her poetry for years. She has given me permission to share these about her great-grandmothers and also about her private prayers to her Lord.

9. Great-Grandmother's Featherbed
By Deborah Sue Hale

My great-grandmother lived in Seminole, Oklahoma…
She lived in what they call a shotgun house…
A one-bedroom house with a small covered porch…
I had cousins that lived in the same town…
We were having a family reunion..
My cousins had a beautiful home…
Everyone spent the night at my cousins except me…
I don't know why I was the lucky one…
But I got to spend the night…
With my great-grandmother…
My mother adored her…
And would tell me stories…
Of how special she was…
She was short in stature and was soft spoken…
She always wore a simple cotton dress…
With an apron ted around her waist…
As the night wore down…
And it was time to go to bed…
She neatly folded down the handmade quilts…
As she turned down the bed…
It revealed beautiful white linen sheets…

I had never seen a feather bed…
And when I laid down on the bed…
It was like floating on a cloud...
As my head sank into the feather pillow
I thought, how cool is this…
I listened to her sweet voice …
Until I fell asleep…
Which didn't take long…
I wouldn't take for that experience…
Getting to sleep in great-grandmother's…
Featherbed…3/11/15

(This was my paternal grandmother, Nora Roberts. A preacher's widow, the mother of six children. I was named after her husband, my grandfather Preacher Albert, until after I was born at home on that snowy night and they discovered I was a girl baby. So they gave me my middle name, Alberta. I would spend time with her during summer vacation. She taught me how to thread a needle and let me brush her waist length gray hair after she let it down from his bun pinned low on his neck.

I, too, slept on that same amazing featherbed as a child. Two other things I remember about it is that when she made it up the next day was, first, she leveled it with a broom handle until it was perfectly flat, and, second, everyone was ordered not to touch it, lean on it, or to be near it during the day. But, oh, that night we could sleep on that cloud once again!)

Tangibles
By Deborah Sue Hale

When I was a little girl we would visit my great-
grandmother…
Mom would set us down on the couch…
And tell us to sit still…
Don't bother anything…
I would sit at attention with my hands folded…
Afraid to move a muscle…
You see she had strategically placed…
All of her treasured dainty, fragile items…
All over the room for people to see…
I felt like I was sitting in the middle of a museum…
Everything on display for the world to see…

But not touch…
Some find comfort in everything having its place…
And they don't want it disturbed…
Get quite upset if misplaced in anyway…
I understand being orderly, neat…
But to be in such a sterile environment…
Like walking into a shrine…
Makes me feel uncomfortable…
I respect their space…
And honor it…
But give me a campfire…
A log to sit on…
A hot cup of coffee…
Moonlight glistening on the ripples…
O a river rushing swiftly by…
Carrying a leaf fallen from a brisk breeze…
The colors of the sky at sunset…
Those are my treasures…
No restrictions…
Just sit back and enjoy…
If I pick up something out of curiosity…
I don't have to carefully place it back…
I can explore it…
Carry it a distance…
And leave it on my way…
For someone else to experience…
I like that… 11/16/14

(This one is about my maternal grandmother, Winnie Myrtle Wilson. Widowed three times and mother of five children. While my sweet Grandmother Roberts was serious and quiet, my grandmother Wilson was full of life, fun, and laughter in spite of her struggles to rear her children alone. I stayed with her during summer vacations and she taught me how to make beautiful crepe paper flowers which she sold for Memorial Day celebrations. Both grandmothers as Christian women added to my rich heritage.)

Be Still

By Deborah Sue Hale

When I shut the door to the stillness of my life…
Closing out the worries of this world…
And hold my presence before the Lord sacred…
My reasoning is silenced…
My arguments are but silly notions…
I justify the logic for conducting my life…
Until that still small voice reveals itself to me…
And I am humbly put in my place…
I can do nothing but listen at that point…
Knowing that the words spoken are absolute truth…
I am at your mercy Lord…
Renew a right spirit within me…
Keep me humble to your presence…
Help me to acknowledge my blessings…
And to realize how grateful I should be…
And whatever fate I am chosen to follow…
Help me to accept it…
Knowing that in due time…
Joy will come in the morning. 12/12/14

Judy Combs Puckett
"Three Men of God"

Dr. Mary Holland
"Mary's Tribute"

Julia Combs de Aquino
Music

Deborah Sue Hale and
Elisabeth Shivers Collett
"Poems about Grandma"

MEMORY LANE PHOTOS

Missionary  *Friends*

Churches

Rev. WT Roberts
(My father)

Berryhill FWB CH
(Where I was saved)

Kingsview FWB Church
OKC

Ministries

Joy Choir

Brazil Children's
Home Sponsors

OASIS

Visits to VA Hospital

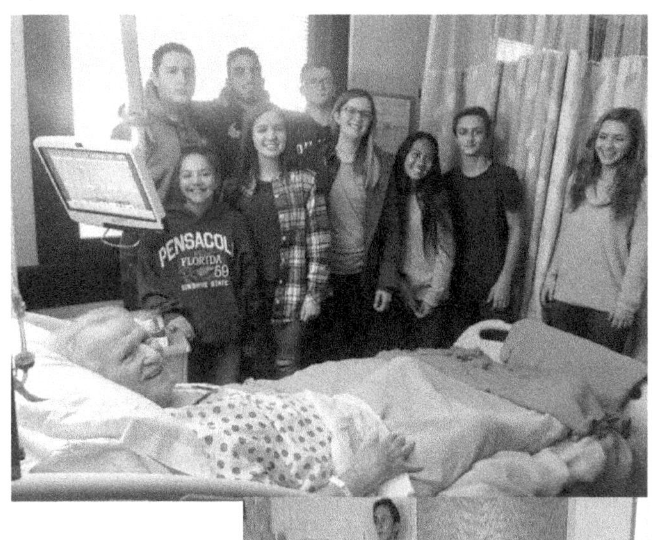

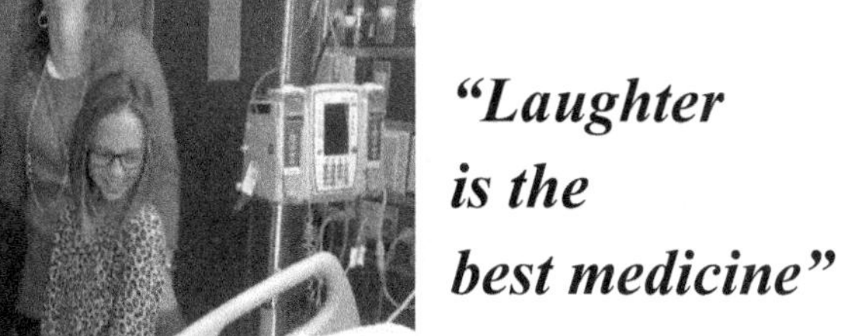

*"Laughter
is the
best medicine"*

Flashback Photos

Jim's headstone was funded by Brazilian FWB Churches

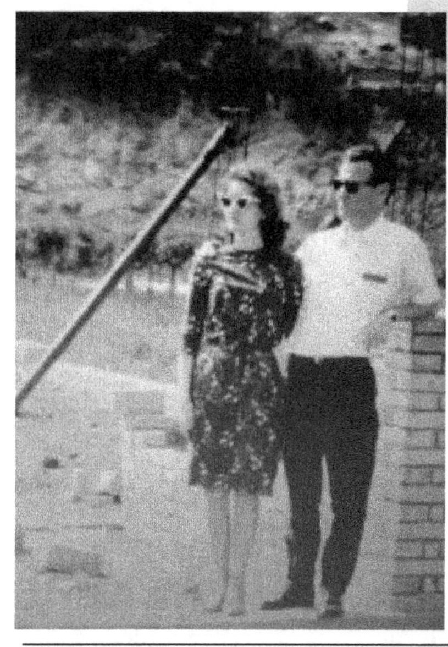

Jim and Shirley looking over building site of Araras church - 1967